Lecture Notes in International Trade

An Undergraduate Course

World Scientific Lecture Notes in Economics and Policy

ISSN: 2630-4872

Series Editor: Ariel Dinar *(University of California, Riverside, USA)*

The World Scientific Lecture Notes in Economics and Policy series is aimed to produce lecture note texts for a wide range of economics disciplines, both theoretical and applied at the undergraduate and graduate levels. Contributors to the series are highly ranked and experienced professors of economics who see in publication of their lectures a mission to disseminate the teaching of economics in an affordable manner to students and other readers interested in enriching their knowledge of economic topics. The series was formerly titled World Scientific Lecture Notes in Economics.

Published:

Vol. 9: *Lecture Notes in International Trade: An Undergraduate Course*
by Priyaranjan Jha

Vol. 8: *Lecture Notes in State and Local Public Finance: (Parts I and II)*
by John Yinger

Vol. 7: *Economics, Game Theory and International Environmental Agreements: The Ca' Foscari Lectures*
by Henry Tulkens

Vol. 6: *Modeling Strategic Behavior: A Graduate Introduction to Game Theory and Mechanism Design*
by George J. Mailath

Vol. 5: *Lecture Notes in Public Budgeting and Financial Management*
by William Duncombe

Vol. 4: *Lecture Notes in Urban Economics and Urban Policy*
by John Yinger

Forthcoming:

Lectures in Neuroeconomics
edited by Paul Glimcher and Hilke Plassmann

For the complete list of volumes in this series, please visit
www.worldscientific.com/series/wslnep

World Scientific Lecture Notes in Economics and Policy – Vol. 9

Lecture Notes in International Trade

An Undergraduate Course

Priyaranjan Jha
University of California, Irvine, USA

World Scientific

NEW JERSEY • LONDON • SINGAPORE • BEIJING • SHANGHAI • HONG KONG • TAIPEI • CHENNAI • TOKYO

Published by

World Scientific Publishing Co. Pte. Ltd.
5 Toh Tuck Link, Singapore 596224
USA office: 27 Warren Street, Suite 401-402, Hackensack, NJ 07601
UK office: 57 Shelton Street, Covent Garden, London WC2H 9HE

Library of Congress Control Number: 2020944318

British Library Cataloguing-in-Publication Data
A catalogue record for this book is available from the British Library.

World Scientific Lecture Notes in Economics and Policy — Vol. 9
LECTURE NOTES IN INTERNATIONAL TRADE
An Undergraduate Course

ISBN 978-981-122-083-8 (hardcover)
ISBN 978-981-122-761-5 (paperback)
ISBN 978-981-122-084-5 (ebook for institutions)
ISBN 978-981-122-085-2 (ebook for individuals)

For any available supplementary material, please visit
https://www.worldscientific.com/worldscibooks/10.1142/11844#t=suppl

Desk Editors: Ramya Gangadharan/Sylvia Koh

Typeset by Stallion Press
Email: enquiries@stallionpress.com

Preface

The very first course in International Trade that I taught was to students of the Masters of International Affairs at Columbia University while I was still a graduate student there. Since joining the University of California, Irvine, in 1997, I have been teaching an undergraduate course in International Trade regularly. This book is based on my lecture notes, which I have refined over time. The book can be used to teach undergraduates and master's students in Business Administration or International and Public Affairs. It would be suitable for a course in International Trade or International Business. The aim is to give students a comprehensive understanding of the relevant topics in International Trade using both economic theory and empirical evidence.

After introducing some key ideas in a textbook on International Trade, this book provides a formal discussion of the Ricardian model of trade, which contains one of the great insights in Economics that what matters for the gains from trade to occur is comparative advantage and not absolute advantage. This is followed by a chapter on the Heckscher–Ohlin model of trade where endowment differences among countries play a key role in determining the pattern of trade. An important result in this chapter is that international trade can produce winners and losers. The next chapter introduces the Krugman model or the model of trade based on internal economies of scale in production. It shows how countries can gain from trade even in a world where countries have identical endowments and technologies, provided that production functions exhibit increasing returns to scale and consumers have a love for variety. Having discussed the most important models of trade in goods, a discussion of the economics of the movements of factors of production — labor and capital — across international borders is provided. The next chapter provides a discussion of the various commercial policy instruments, such as tariffs, quotas and export subsidies, that countries use to intervene in trade. This is followed up by a discussion of the arguments for and against intervening in trade. While the policy discussions in this chapter are based on the aggregate welfare of society, the next chapter introduces the process of actual policymaking in democratic societies, which takes us into the realm of political economy. The focus here is on the political economy of trade policy. This is followed up by a discussion of the economics of preferential trading agreements, and the concluding chapter provides a history of multilateral trading agreements under the aegis of GATT (General Agreement on Tariffs and Trade) and its evolution into the World Trade Organization (WTO).

About the Author

Priyaranjan Jha is a Professor of Economics at the University of California, Irvine. He did a B.A. in Economics from St. Stephen's College, Delhi, a M.A. in Economics from the Delhi School of Economics and a Ph.D. in Economics from Columbia University. His areas of research are International Trade and Economic Growth and Development. He has published a large number of papers in peer-reviewed journals such as *The Economic Journal*, the *Journal of International Economics*, the *Journal of Development Economics*, the *European Economic Review*, the *Journal of Applied Econometrics* and *The World Economy*. He has also served on the board of editors of several journals. Currently, he serves as a co-editor of the *Indian Growth and Development Review* and an associate editor of the *Journal of Development Economics*. He also writes for popular media outlets, such as *The Economic Times* and *The Indian Express*.

Acknowledgments

I would like to thank the undergraduate students at the University of California, Irvine, who have taken a course in International Trade with me and have given me the opportunity to teach them as well as learn from them. My children, Aastha and Ashaank, deserve special thanks for helping type up the manuscript based on my scattered lecture notes. Finally, I would like to thank my wife, Bharati, for her sustained support through the years.

Contents

Chapter 1

Introduction

The aim of this book is to introduce undergraduate students to the economics of international trade. When we say international trade, what we mean is the exchange of goods and services across international borders. When a Chinese firm Lenovo ships a laptop computer to the United States, it is the export of a good by China to the US. When a Chinese airline buys an aircraft from Boeing, it is the import of a good by China from the US. One way to see the importance of international trade for the world economy is to see how large the exports are relative to the GDP for the world. The GDP for the world captures the total amount of economic activity for the world in a year. The exports capture the total amount of goods exported by each country in the world. Figure 1.1 (based on the data from the World Bank) shows that the Export–GDP ratio for the world has increased from about 12% in 1960 to about 30% in 2017. That is, there has been a substantial increase in world trade over the last 60 years. The ratio for the world masks enormous variations across countries. For example, in the latest year, this ratio was 87% for a small European country like Belgium but only 12% for the US. For China, it was 19.5%. In general, smaller countries trade a larger fraction of their GDP than larger countries; however, even controlling for country size, there are enormous variations across countries.

If we go back in time, we realize that there was a tremendous growth in world trade during the period 1870–1913. This was followed by a dramatic reversal in the world trade during the inter-war years,

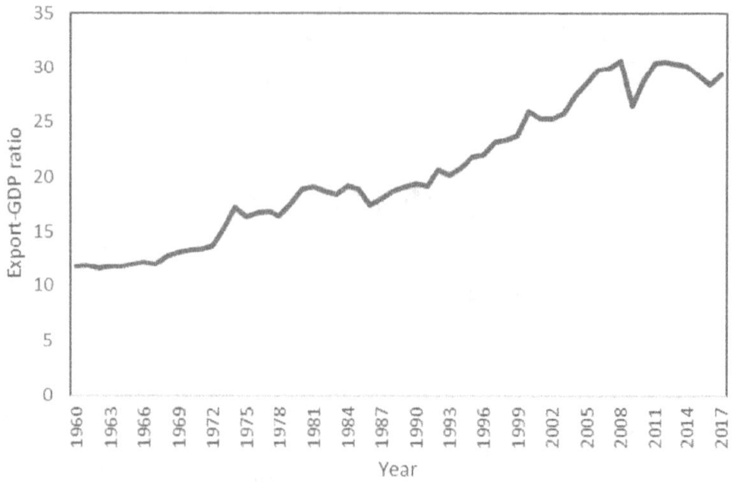

Figure 1.1: Exports to GDP ratio for the world.

Table 1.1: Historical pattern of export–GDP ratio for the world.

1870	4.6
1913	7.9
1950	5.5
1973	10.5
1998	17.2

Source: Angus Maddison, The World Economy: A Millennial Perspective, World Bank, 2001.

and it was only after the end of the Second World War that global trade started increasing again. This historical pattern is apparent from the data from Maddison (2001) shown in Table 1.1.

The sustained growth in world trade since the end of the Second World War has been accompanied by a changing pattern of trade. While in the late 19th and early 20th centuries, a lot of trade involved exchange of manufactured goods for agricultural products, the trade now is dominated by two-way exchange of manufactured products.

This is true not only of trade among developed countries but also of trade between developed and developing countries. For example, more than 90% of the exports of China, a developing country and a relatively recent entrant to the world trade, consist of manufactured goods.

In this book, we study the determinants of the pattern of trade among countries and also analyze how trade can provide aggregate gains to a country and at the same time produce winners and losers. That is, not everyone in a country is guaranteed to gain from international trade and to ensure that gains from trade are distributed in the entire population, governments may have to undertake fiscal transfers. In addition to studying the trade in goods and services, we also study the economics of the movement of factors of production such as labor and capital across international borders. From the news headlines, it is clear that countries use commercial policy instruments such as tariffs, quotas and export subsidies to impede or promote trade. We study the welfare implications of these commercial policy instruments and also analyze the welfare implications of preferential trading agreements signed by a subset of countries. We see that countries do not always adopt policies which increase aggregate welfare. Why? The answer to this question will take us into a discussion of the political economy of trade policy. Finally, we conclude with a discussion of the history of multilateral trade agreements since the end of the Second World War culminating in the formation of the World Trade Organization.

The structure of the book is as follows. In Chapter 2, we introduce the Ricardian model of international trade which states that the main reason why countries trade is that different countries have different productivities (or technologies) for producing different goods and services. It shows how countries can gain from exporting goods that they are relatively better at making and importing goods that they are relatively worse at making. Chapter 3 discusses the Heckscher–Ohlin model of trade where endowment differences among countries play a key role in determining the pattern of trade. An important conclusion of this chapter is that international trade can produce winners and losers. That is, even though there are aggregate gains from trade, some factors of production gain while others lose. Chapter 4 introduces the Krugman model or the model of trade based on internal economies of scale in production. It shows how countries can gain from trade even in a world where countries have identical endowments and technologies, provided that production functions exhibit increasing returns to scale and consumers have a love for variety. Since increasing returns to scale gives rise to an imperfectly competitive market structure, we also discuss the economics of dumping. Having discussed various models of trade in goods, Chapter 5 discusses the economics of the movements of factors of production. In particular, it analyzes the implications of movements of labor and capital across borders. Chapter 6 discusses the welfare implications of intervention in trade. That is, it provides a discussion of the various commercial policy instruments, such as tariffs, quotas and export subsidies, that countries use to intervene in trade. Chapter 7 examines various arguments for and against intervention in trade. While the welfare implications in Chapters 6 and 7 are based on the aggregate welfare of society, Chapter 8 introduces the process of actual policymaking in democratic societies, which takes us into the realm of political economy. The focus here is on the political economy of trade policy. Chapter 9 discusses the economics of preferential trading agreements, while Chapter 10 provides a history of multilateral trading agreements under the aegis of the General Agreement on Tariffs and Trade (GATT) and its evolution into the World Trade Organization (WTO).

Chapter 2

The Ricardian Model

2.1 Introduction

In his book titled *On the Principles of Political Economy and Taxation* published in 1817, David Ricardo discussed the theory of comparative advantage, which is one of the great insights in Economics. The Ricardian theory of comparative advantage is based on the idea that if there are technological differences in the production of goods across countries, then countries can gain from trade by exporting goods for which the country has a lower opportunity cost of production and importing goods for which the country's opportunity costs of production are higher. The model can be understood using a two-country, two-good and one factor of production example.

Suppose that the two countries are Home and Foreign and the two goods are Bread and Cloth. The lone factor of production is labor. The production of one unit of each good in each country requires a certain amount of labor which is called the unit labor requirement. Denote the unit labor requirement in Home by a_{Li}, where $i = B, C$, and B denotes Bread and C denotes Cloth.

Denote the unit labor requirement in Foreign by a^*_{Li}. To fix ideas, let us work with the following numbers.

That is, $a_{LB} = 1$, $a_{LC} = 2$, $a^*_{LB} = 4$ and $a^*_{LC} = 3$. Denote the total amount of labor in Home by L and the total amount of labor in Foreign by L^*. For later use, also assume that $L = L^* = 600$.

Given the information above, it is easily verified that Home is better at making both Bread and Cloth because Home requires less labor to produce a unit of Bread and a unit Cloth compared to Foreign. In other words, Home labor is more productive than Foreign in the production of both goods. Thus, Home has an absolute advantage in the production of both Bread and Cloth.

The genius of Ricardo lay in showing that the two countries could still gain from trade. To understand this, we need to bring in the concept of opportunity cost. Recall that the opportunity cost of producing a good is the next best alternative foregone. Note that when Home produces one unit of Bread, it uses one unit of labor. The alternative use of labor in Home is to produce Cloth. How much Cloth can one unit of labor in Home produce? The answer is 1/2, because each unit of Cloth requires two units of labor; therefore, one unit of labor can produce only 1/2 Cloth. Thus, the opportunity cost of producing Bread in Home is 1/2 Cloth. The flip side of this is that the opportunity cost of producing Cloth in Home is two units of Bread. Doing the same exercise for Foreign verifies the fact that the opportunity cost of producing Bread in Foreign is 4/3 Cloth, and the opportunity cost of producing Cloth in Foreign is 3/4 Bread. From the above exercise, we conclude that the opportunity cost of producing Bread is lower in Home (1/2 Cloth vs 4/3 Cloth in Foreign), whereas the opportunity cost of producing Cloth is lower in Foreign (3/4 Bread vs 2 Bread in Home). Therefore, Home has a comparative advantage in Bread and Foreign has a comparative advantage in Cloth and the two countries can gain by engaging in trade.

To see how the two countries can gain from trade, suppose that Home offers Foreign the following deal. Let us exchange 1 Bread for 1 Cloth. That is, Home offers Foreign 1 Bread in exchange for 1 Cloth. If Home has to produce Cloth domestically, it has to give up 2 Bread to get 1 Cloth, but with international trade with Foreign it can get 1 Cloth in exchange for 1 Bread. Therefore, it is cheaper for Home to import Cloth than to produce it domestically. Similarly, Foreign has to give up 4/3 Cloth to get 1 Bread in autarky, where we use the word autarky to denote a situation when a country is not trading. But Foreign can get 1 Bread in exchange for 1 Cloth by trading with Home. What we have shown is that it is cheaper for Home to import Cloth from Foreign and it is cheaper for Foreign to import Bread from Home compared to producing them domestically. This is how countries gain from trade: It is cheaper for them to import some goods than to produce them domestically. It is "as if" trade with Foreign is giving Home a better technology to produce Cloth and Foreign a better technology to produce Bread. It is worth reiterating that the countries can gain from trade even though Home is better at producing both goods and Foreign is worse at producing both goods.

In the above discussion, we simply assumed that Bread and Cloth are exchanged one for one in the world market. However, that is only one possible exchange rate between Bread and Cloth. Below, we are going to derive the rate at which the two goods will be exchanged in the world market.

2.2 Autarky Equilibrium

Let us first derive the autarky equilibrium in each country. We will discuss it in detail for Home and the same analysis will apply *mutatis mutandis* to Foreign. We assume that both goods and labor markets are perfectly competitive. Moreover, workers are freely mobile within a country but immobile across countries. Denote the nominal wage in Home by w. When we say "nominal", we mean in terms of some currency, say in terms of the local currency USD in the US. What is the nominal cost of producing a unit of Bread in Home? Since a_{LB} units of labor are required to produce one unit of Bread, the cost of producing a unit of Bread is wa_{LB}. Similarly, the cost of producing a unit of Cloth in Home is wa_{LC}. Denote the nominal price of Bread in Home by P_B and the nominal price of Cloth by P_C. Define the relative price of Bread, price of Bread in terms of Cloth, as $\frac{P_B}{P_C}$. Now, perfect competition in the goods market implies that the price of producing a good must equal the average cost (also equal to marginal cost): $P_B = wa_{LB}$. Similarly, $P_C = wa_{LC}$. The two together imply that the relative price of Bread $\frac{P_B}{P_C}$ equals $\frac{a_{LB}}{a_{LC}}$. Given the numbers in Table 2.1, the relative price of Bread in Home equals 1/2, which is

Table 2.1: Unit labor requirements.

	Home	Foreign
Bread	1	4
Cloth	2	3

simply the opportunity cost of Bread in terms of Cloth. That is, in autarky equilibrium in Home, one unit of Bread will be exchanged for 1/2 Cloth.

We can derive the relative price of Bread in Home in an alternative way which is useful in deriving the world equilibrium later. What should be the nominal wage in Bread production in Home? Remember that both goods and labor market are competitive; therefore, the wage of a worker should equal the value of the marginal product. Now, if a_{LB} units of labor are required to produce one unit of Bread in Home, one unit of labor can produce $\frac{1}{a_{LB}}$ units of Bread. That is, the productivity of labor is simply the inverse of the unit labor requirement. Therefore, the value of the marginal product of the labor in Bread production equals $P_B\frac{1}{a_{LB}}$. Hence, the wage in Bread production must equal $P_B\frac{1}{a_{LB}}$. Similarly, the wage in Cloth production must equal $P_C\frac{1}{a_{LC}}$. What would happen if $P_B\frac{1}{a_{LB}} > P_C\frac{1}{a_{LC}}$? Since the wage is higher in Bread production, all workers would want to work in Bread production and no Cloth will be produced. In the reverse case, all workers would want to work in Cloth production and no Bread will be produced. Therefore, in order for both Bread and Cloth to be produced, the following must be true: $P_B\frac{1}{a_{LB}} = P_C\frac{1}{a_{LC}}$. This again yields $\frac{P_B}{P_C} = \frac{a_{LB}}{a_{LC}}$. In deriving this result in the current paragraph, we have used the assumption of free mobility of labor. Free mobility of labor implies that wages must be equalized in the two sectors: $w = P_B\frac{1}{a_{LB}} = P_C\frac{1}{a_{LC}}$.

We can depict the autarky equilibrium using the production possibility frontier (PPF here-after) and indifference curves. Given that Home has L units of labor, if Home devotes all its labor to Bread production, it can produce L/a_{LB} units of Bread. Similarly, if it devotes all its labor to Cloth production, it can produce L/a_{LC} units of Cloth. Given the numbers in Table 2.1, Home can produce a maximum of 600 units of Bread and a maximum of 300 units of Cloth. These are the two end points of the PPF in the (Bread, Cloth) space. Now starting at 600 units of Bread, if Home reduces the production of Bread by one unit, how much Cloth can it produce? Since Home will be withdrawing one unit of labor away from Bread production, the amount of Cloth produced will be exactly 1/2. Therefore, every time Home reduces production of Bread by a unit, it can get 1/2 more Cloth. Therefore, the various combinations of Bread and Cloth that Home can produce are given by the straight line joining (600,0) to (0,300) in the (Bread, Cloth) space. This line has a slope of $-\frac{a_{LB}}{a_{LC}} = \frac{1}{2}$, the absolute value of which is the opportunity cost of producing Bread in Home. We depict the PPF of Home in Figure 2.1.

While the PPF captures all combinations of Bread and Cloth that Home can produce given its endowment of labor and the technology to produce Bread and Cloth, which combination does Home actually produce? To determine this, we need to bring in the preferences of Home consumers between Bread and Cloth. The preferences can be captured using indifference curves. Assuming that all consumers

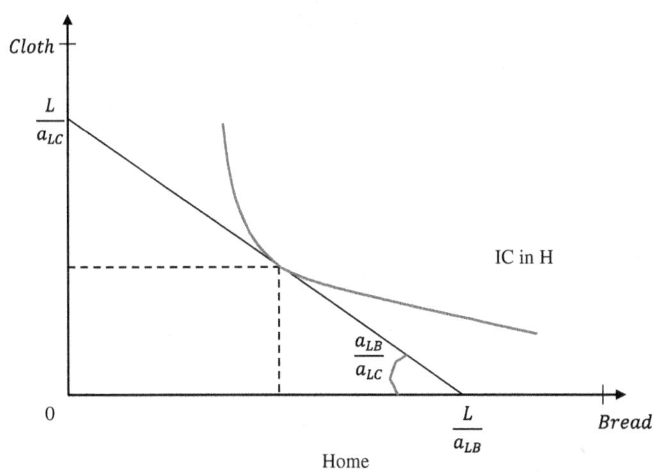

Figure 2.1: Autarky equilibrium in home.

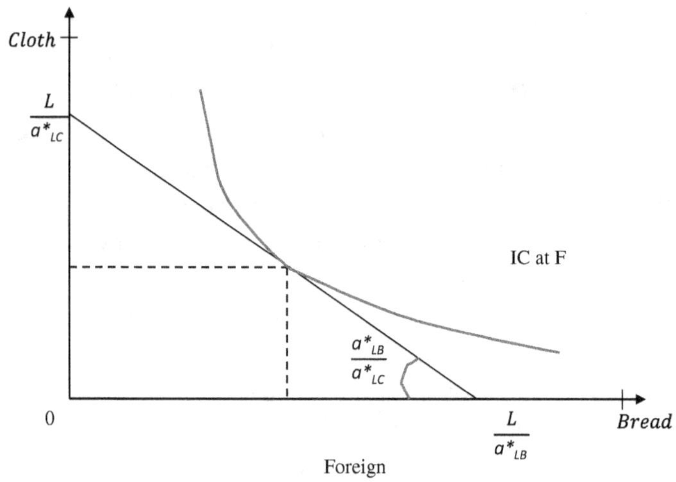

Figure 2.2: Autarky equilibrium in foreign.

in Home have identical preferences, we can use a representative consumer's indifference map to depict preferences. Superimposing the indifference map in Figure 2.1, we can find the highest possible indifference curve compatible with the PPF in Figure 2.1. This will be given by the indifference curve which is tangent to the PPF. The point of tangency between the indifference curve and the PPF will determine the amounts of Bread and Cloth produced and consumed in Home in autarky. Irrespective of the point of tangency, the relative price of Bread in Home will be 1/2 in our numerical example and will be independent of the preferences. This is a special feature of the model where the relative price is independent of the preferences because of the linearity of the PPF.

We can determine the autarky equilibrium in Foreign in an analogous fashion and the equilibrium is shown in Figure 2.2.

The slope of the PPF in Foreign equals 4/3 (in our numerical example and $\frac{a^*_{LB}}{a^*_{LC}}$ more generally), which is the opportunity cost of producing Bread in Foreign.

2.3 Trading Equilibrium

Having determined the autarky equilibrium in the two countries, we turn our attention to the world equilibrium or the trading equilibrium. We assume no trade restrictions, that is, countries can trade the two goods freely. The first question we want to answer is at what rate will the two goods be exchanged in a trading equilibrium. Recall from our discussion earlier that the relative price of Bread in autarky in Home is 1/2, whereas in Foreign it is 4/3. That is, one Bread is exchanged for 1/2 Cloth in Home and 4/3 Cloth in Foreign. We are going to find the world relative price of Bread by deriving the world relative supply and world relative demand for Bread. All the action is going to be in deriving the relative supply.

2.3.1 *World relative supply curve*

The world relative supply of Bread is the sum of Bread produced in Home and Foreign divided by the sum of Cloth produced in Home and Foreign: $RS_B = \frac{Q_B+Q_B^*}{Q_C+Q_C^*}$, where Q_i is the amount of good-i produced in Home and Q_i^* is the amount of good-i produced in Foreign. Let us derive the relative supply of Bread for various relative prices of Bread.

- **When $(\frac{P_B}{P_C}) \in$ (0,1/2):** Let us start with a relative price of Bread of 1/4. How much Bread will be produced in Home at this relative price? Recall that the opportunity cost of Bread in Home, is 1/2. Therefore, the relative price is less than the opportunity cost, and hence no Bread will be produced in Home. To understand why no Bread is produced in Home at a relative price of 1/4 in an alternative way, recall from our discussion of wages earlier that for the wages to be identical in Bread and Cloth production, the following must be true: $P_B\frac{1}{a_{LB}} = P_C\frac{1}{a_{LC}}$. When $\frac{P_B}{P_C} = \frac{1}{4}$, it is less than $\frac{a_{LB}}{a_{LC}} = \frac{1}{2}$. That is, we are in a situation of $P_B\frac{1}{a_{LB}} < P_C\frac{1}{a_{LC}}$ or the wage in Bread production is less than the wage in Cloth production, and hence all workers would want to work in Cloth production in Home. Therefore, the production of Bread in Home is zero. Since $\frac{P_B}{P_C} = \frac{1}{4} < \frac{a_{LB}^*}{a_{LC}^*} = \frac{2}{3}$, the relative price of Bread is less than the opportunity cost of Bread in Foreign as well. Therefore, there is no Bread production in either country. That is, $RS_B = 0$ since the numerator is zero. The logic used in this paragraph holds for any relative price of Bread less than 1/2. Therefore, we have derived the first segment of our world relative supply curve which coincides with the vertical axis for any relative price less than $\frac{1}{2}$.

- **When** $(\frac{P_B}{P_C}) = 1/2$**:** What if the world relative price of Bread equals 1/2? This corresponds to the autarky relative price of Bread in Home, which corresponds to the opportunity cost of Bread in Home. We have seen earlier that this is also the slope of the PPF of Home. Therefore, Home can produce any amount of Bread and Cloth on its PPF. Therefore, the amount of Bread and Cloth produced at Home can vary from (600,0) to (0,300). Since the relative price of 1/2 is still less than the opportunity cost of 2/3 in Foreign, it does not produce any Bread. Foreign produces only Cloth at this relative price. Therefore, the relative supply of Bread in the world varies between 0 (when Home is producing $(0, 300)$) and 3, where 3 is obtained when Home produces only Bread and Foreign produces only Cloth, giving $Q_B = 600, Q_B^* = 0, Q_C = 200$ and $Q_C^* = 0$. Therefore, at $(\frac{P_B}{P_C}) = 1/2$, the world relative supply curve has a horizontal segment going from 0 to 3.
- **When** $(\frac{P_B}{P_C}) \in (1/2, 4/3)$**:** It should be clear by now that if the relative price of Bread exceeds 1/2, then Home will produce only Bread because the relative price of Bread is greater than the opportunity cost of Bread and the flip side of it is that the relative price of Cloth is less than the opportunity cost of Cloth. Since the opportunity cost of Bread in Foreign is 4/3, as long as $\frac{P_B}{P_C} < 4/3$, Foreign does not produce any Bread. Therefore, in this range of relative price, Home produces only Bread and Foreign produces only Cloth, and hence the relative supply of Bread is 3. Thus, the world relative supply curve has a vertical segment in this range.
- **When** $(\frac{P_B}{P_C}) < 4/3$: When the relative price of Bread hits 4/3, it becomes equal to the opportunity cost of Bread in Foreign. Therefore, now Foreign can produce any amount of Bread and Cloth on its PPF as shown in Figure 2.2. In particular, Foreign can produce any amount of Cloth from a minimum of 0 to a maximum of 200. Since Home is producing only Bread, when Foreign produces 0 Cloth, the worldwide production of Cloth becomes 0, and hence the world relative supply of Bread becomes infinity because the denominator is 0. When Foreign produces

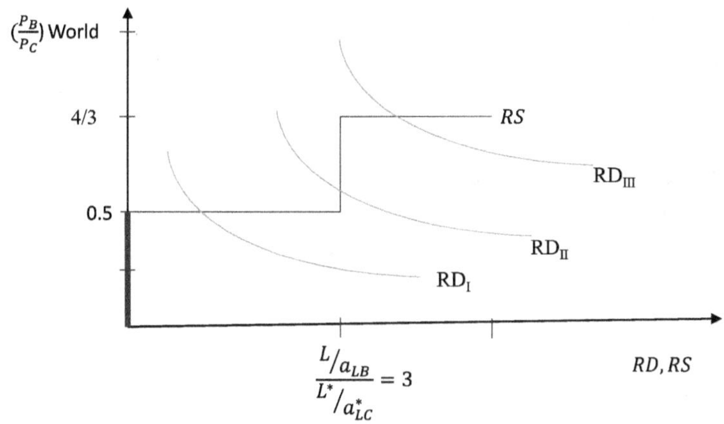

Graph of relative demand and supply given world relative prices

Figure 2.3: World equilibrium.

only Cloth, then the world relative supply of Bread attains its minimum value of 3. Therefore, the relative supply of Bread can be anything between 3 and infinity. Hence, it has a horizontal segment at $\frac{P_B}{P_C} = 4/3$ stretching to infinity.

If the relative price of Bread is greater than 4/3, then Foreign produces only Bread as well because the opportunity of Cloth exceeds the relative price of Cloth. Therefore, there is no production of Cloth worldwide, and hence the relative supply of Bread is infinity for any relative price in excess of 2/3. In a way, the relative supply curve does not exist for $\frac{P_B}{P_C} > 4/3$.

The step-wise relative supply curve derived above is depicted in Figure 2.3.

2.3.2 *World equilibrium*

The relative demand for Bread will simply be a decreasing function of the relative price of Bread. Since preferences are identical across countries, both countries will have the same relative demand for Bread, and hence the world relative demand (which is a weighted average of the relative demands in the two countries) will be identical to the relative demands in the two countries.

The world equilibrium relative price will be determined by the intersection of the world relative demand and world relative supply curves. Depending on the position of the world relative demand curve, we can discuss three possible cases.

- **Case I.** In this case, the world relative demand curve labeled RD_I intersects the world relative supply curve on the first horizontal segment. Therefore, the equilibrium world relative price is 1/2. Recall from the discussion of the relative supply curve earlier that Foreign does not produce any Bread at this price. That is, Foreign produces only Cloth. Since the equilibrium relative price corresponds to the autarky relative price in Home, Home produces both Bread and Cloth. This is the pattern of production that obviously results in Home exporting Bread and Foreign exporting Cloth. Therefore, in Case I, the production pattern is one where Home is diversified (producing both Bread and Cloth), whereas Foreign is completely specialized in the production of Cloth. The pattern of trade is determined by the pattern of comparative advantage which leads Home to export Bread and Foreign to export Cloth.
- **Case II.** In this case, the relative demand curve labeled RD_{II} intersects the relative supply curve in the vertical segment between 1/2 and 4/3. Therefore, the equilibrium world relative price settles between 1/2 and 4/3 as well. Recall from the discussion of the relative supply curve that at this relative price, Home produces only Bread and Foreign produces only Cloth, giving a relative supply of 3. That is, both countries are completely specialized in production: Home in Bread and Foreign in Cloth. The reason is that the relative price of Bread exceeds the opportunity cost of Bread in Home and the relative price of Cloth exceeds the opportunity cost of Cloth in Foreign. The pattern of trade is same as in Case I: Home exports Bread and Foreign exports Cloth.
- **Case III.** In this case, the relative demand curve labeled RD_{III} intersects the relative supply curve at the second horizontal segment, and therefore the equilibrium world relative price becomes 4/3. At this relative price, Home is completely specialized in the production of Bread as in Case II, but Foreign becomes

diversified. Since the equilibrium world relative price corresponds to the autarky relative price in Foreign, it produces both Bread and Cloth. The pattern of trade is again one where Home exports Bread and Foreign exports Cloth.

While the pattern of production and the equilibrium relative price of Bread differ in the various trading equilibria discussed earlier, the pattern of trade remains the same in all cases and is determined by the pattern of comparative advantage which is independent of the demand conditions. Having determined the world equilibrium, we next turn our attention to the important issue of gains from trade.

2.4 Gains from Trade

The gains from trade can be discussed in several ways. It has already been done in one simple way by comparing the autarky relative price with the world relative price. To see this clearly, suppose that the trading equilibrium is of the type discussed in Case II above and the world relative price settles at 1. That is, one Bread exchanges for one Cloth in the world market. The gain to Home comes from the fact that in autarky it had to give up 2 Bread to get 1 Cloth, but now it is has to give up only 1 Bread to get 1 Cloth. Similarly, Foreign had to give up 4/3 Cloth to get 1 Bread in autarky. Now, it has to give up only 1 Cloth to get 1 Bread. Therefore, it is cheaper for Home to import Cloth than to produce it domestically and cheaper for Foreign to import Bread than to produce it domestically. What if we are in Case I instead? Now, the world price corresponds to the autarky price, and hence there are no gains from trade for Home. For Foreign there are gains because at a world price of 1/2, Foreign has to give up only 1/2 Cloth to get 1 Bread, while in autarky it had to give up 4/3 Cloth. Similarly, in Case III, only Home gains because the world price corresponds to the autarky relative price in Foreign. Given the world relative price of 4/3, Home has to give up only 3/4 Bread to get 1 Cloth, while in autarky it had to give up two Bread. The result that only one country gains from trade in some cases is limited to the two-good Ricardian model; later, when we extend it to the many-goods case, we will see that, in general, both countries gain from trade.

Another way to see the gains from trade is to look at the real wages in the two countries before and after trade. The real wages are expressed in terms of goods that can be bought in exchange for a unit of labor. The autarky real wages in the two countries will be simply the inverses of the numbers in Table 2.1. In Home, the real wage in terms of Bread is 1 because one unit of labor produces 1 Bread. Similarly, the real wage in Home in terms of Cloth is 1/2 because one unit of labor can produce only 1/2 Cloth. Similarly, in Foreign, the real wages are 1/4 Bread and 1/3 Cloth. The post-trade real wage depends on where the world price settles. Let us discuss it first for the case when the world relative price settles at 1. That is, 1 Bread is exchanged for 1 Cloth. Since Home is completely specialized in the production of Bread this world price, Home real wage in terms of Bread remains 1. However, Home workers can exchange 1 Bread for 1 Cloth in the world market; therefore, the real wage in terms of Cloth goes up from 1/2 to 1. Similarly, Foreign is going to be completely specialized in Cloth production. Therefore, the real wage in terms of Cloth remains unchanged from autarky at 1/3. However, Foreign workers can exchange one Cloth for one Bread, and therefore their real wage in terms of Bread becomes 1/3. That is, the real wage in terms of Bread increases from 1/4 to 1/3. It should be obvious from the argument presented here that real wage gains will take place only if the world relative price differs from the autarky relative price. Therefore, in Case I, only Foreign will experience real wage gains and in Case III, only Home will experience real wage gains.

Yet another way the gains from trade can be demonstrated is by using the PPF shown in Figures 2.1 and 2.2. In autarky, the PPF is also the consumption possibility frontier (CPF) of the country. That is, a country will both produce and consume on the PPF. After opening up to trade, things can change. Let us look at Home in the case when the world relative price of Bread settles at 1. In this case, Home can produce 600 Bread by completely specializing in the production of Bread, and given the exchange rate it, can potentially exchange 600 Bread for 600 Cloth.[1] Therefore, the new consumption possibility frontier for Home as shown in Figure 2.4(a) is the line connecting 600 Bread to 600 Cloth.

The gap between the PPF and the new CPF, the shaded area, can be thought of as the new consumption possibilities that arose due to trade. This area was not available in autarky. In terms of the indifference curves, in autarky the highest possible indifference curve Home could achieve was IC_{Autarky}, but in the post-trade situation the highest possible indifference curve is IC_{Trade}.

Similarly, in Figure 2.4(b) Foreign's CPF expands to one connecting 200 Bread with 200 Cloth and the shaded area captures the new consumption possibilities for Foreign. Again, for the CPF to expand beyond the PPF, the world relative price must differ from the autarky relative price, and therefore only Foreign will gain in Case I discussed earlier and only Home will gain in Case III. In terms of the indifference curves, in autarky the highest possible indifference curve Foreign could achieve was IC_{Autarky}, but in the post-trade situation the highest possible indifference curve is IC_{Trade}.

Having discussed the two-good Ricardian model, we next turn our attention to the many-goods case.[2]

2.5 Many-Goods Ricardian Model

Now, suppose that instead of there being just two goods, the two countries Home and Foreign can produce six goods, and the unit labor requirements for the six goods are given in Table 2.2.

The last column of Table 2.2 is the ratio of Foreign unit labor requirement to Home unit labor requirement. Since the productivity

---

[1]Strictly speaking, since Foreign can produce a maximum of 200 Cloth, if Home and Foreign are the only two countries in the world, Home can buy a maximum of 200 Cloth. But the argument here is more general about the possibilities. That is, suppose that Home was a small country and there were a large number of countries producing Bread and Cloth in the world. If they exchanged one for one in the world market, Home could then potentially exchange 600 Bread for 600 Cloth.

[2]The many goods case was originally discussed by Dornbusch, R., Fischer, S., and Samuelson, P. (1977). Comparative advantage, trade, and payments in a ricardian model with a continuum of goods, *The American Economic Review.*

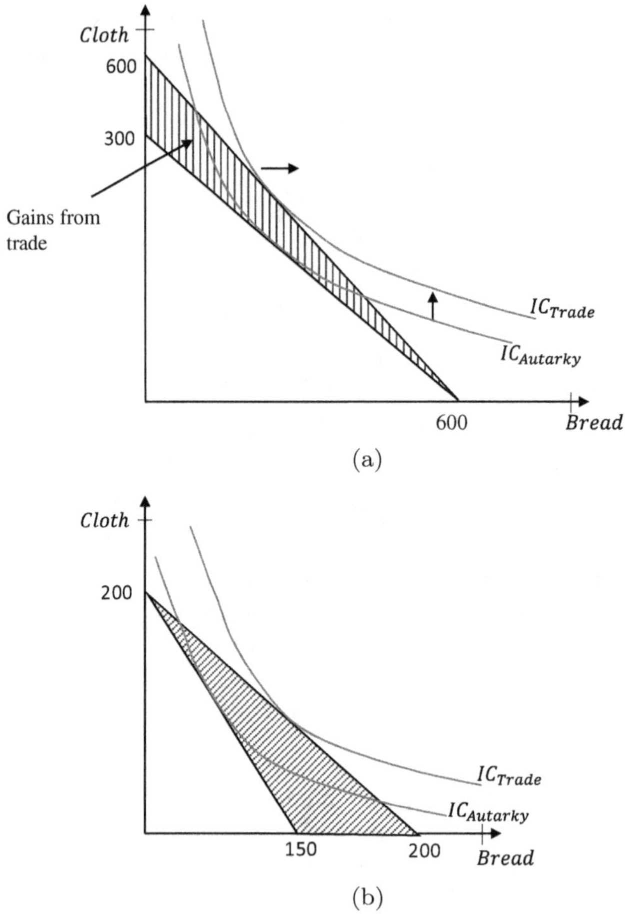

Figure 2.4: (a) Gains from trade for Home; (b) Gains from trade in Foreign.

of a worker is simply the inverse of the unit labor requirement, this ratio captures Home's productivity relative to Foreign's productivity. From Table 2.2, note that Home has an absolute productivity advantage in all six goods. In fact, we have named goods in such a way that Home's productivity advantage is highest in good A(15 times) and lowest in good F (twice). The question is how to determine

---

Our exposition below follows a simplified version in Krugman, P., Obstfeld, M., and Melitz, M. 2018. *International Economics* (11th edition), Pearson, chapter 3.

Table 2.2: Many-goods Ricardian example.

Goods	Home (a_{Li})	Foreign (a^*_{Li})	Productivity ratio ($\frac{a^*_{Li}}{a_{Li}}$)
A	1	15	15
B	5	60	12
C	4	40	10
D	3	24	8
E	7	21	3
F	8	16	2

comparative advantage in this multi-goods case. As in the two-good case, denote the nominal wage in Home by w and that in Foreign by w^* in units of some common currency. Given the unit labor requirements, the cost of producing a good is simply the wage rate multiplied by the unit labor requirement, and given perfectly competitive goods markets, this must equal the price as well. That is, the price of good-i in Home is $p_i = a_{Li}w$ and the price in Foreign is $p^*_i = a^*_{Li}w^*$. Now, in order for Home to have a comparative advantage in good i, the following inequality must hold: $p_i < p^*_i$ or $a_{Li}\,w < a^*_{Li}w^*$ or $\frac{w}{w*} < \frac{a^*_{Li}}{a_{Li}}$. The last inequality has an intuitive appeal. For example, suppose that the Home wage is seven times Foreign's wage. Now, in order for Home to have a comparative advantage in a good, its productivity should be at least seven times Foreign's productivity. Given the numbers in Table 2.2, if the Home wage is seven times the Foreign wage, then Home will have a comparative advantage in goods A, B, C and D and Foreign in E and F. The general point is that if we know $\frac{w}{w*}$ ratio, we can determine the pattern of comparative advantage given the numbers in Table 2.2. We turn to the determination of Home wage relative to Foreign wage $\frac{w}{w*}$, next.

The relative wage, $\frac{w}{w*}$, is going to be determined by the relative demand and relative supply of Home labor. The supply of Home labor relative to Foreign labor is as before. That is, if the total amount of Home labor is L and the total amount of Foreign labor is L^*, then the

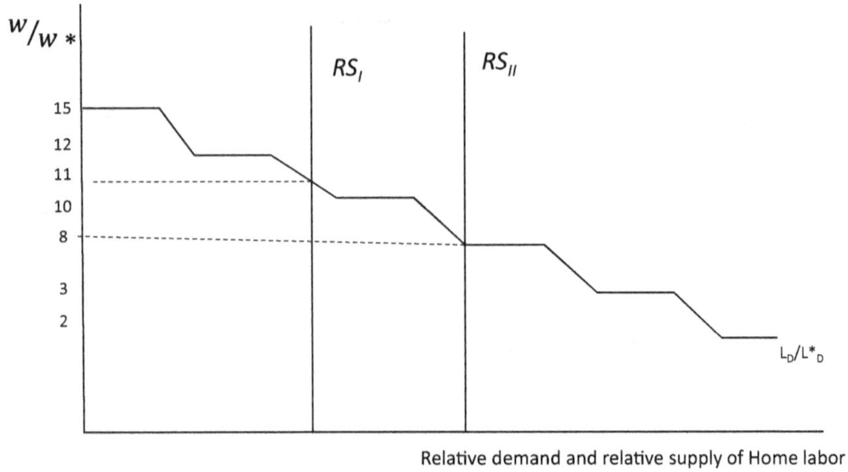

Figure 2.5: Many-goods Ricardian model.

relative supply of Home labor is inelastically given by $\frac{L}{L*}$. Therefore, in Figure 2.5, the relative supply of Home labor as a function of Home relative wage is a vertical line.

The relative demand for Home labor is a little more complicated and will be derived in several steps. Suppose that $\frac{w}{w*} = 16$. It is clear from Table 2.2 that Home cannot compete in any good at this relative wage, and therefore there is no demand for Home labor. The flip side of this is that Foreign has a comparative advantage in all six goods and that will generate demand for Foreign labor. Therefore, the relative demand for Home labor is zero when $\frac{w}{w*} = 16$. This argument holds for any relative wage greater than 15. Therefore, the relative demand for Home labor corresponds to the vertical axis for $\frac{w}{w*} > 15$. What if $\frac{w}{w*} = 15$? Now, Home becomes competitive in good A because $\frac{a^*_{LA}}{a_{LA}} = 15$, and hence $p_A = a_{LA}w = p^*_A = a^*_{LA}w^*$. Since the cost of good A is the same in both countries, both are equally good at producing good A. Home cannot compete in any other good given such a high relative wage. Since both are equally good at producing good A, there is some indeterminacy in the production of good A. In particular, Home can produce any amount of good A from zero to the total demanded by both countries and consequently the demand for Home labor is anything between zero and what is required to produce all of good A in the world. Thus, the relative demand for Home labor has a horizontal segment at $\frac{w}{w*} = 15$. Now, suppose that the relative wage falls below 15 but remains above $12 : \frac{w}{w*} \in (12, 15)$. In this case, Home will have a comparative advantage in good A and Foreign will have a comparative advantage in goods B through F. Now, the demand for Home labor comes from the production of good A for both countries, whereas the demand for Foreign labor comes from goods B through E which are produced for both countries. This pattern of comparative advantage is going to hold for any relative wage $\frac{w}{w*} \in (12, 15)$. However, in Figure 2.5, the relative demand for Home labor has a downward sloping segment in this range. The reason is that as $\frac{w}{w*}$ falls, albeit staying in the range (12, 15), the cost of producing good A falls and this leads to an increase in demand for good A, causing an increased demand for Home labor. Once relative wage falls to 12, Home becomes competitive in good B as well, and therefore the demand for Home labor comes from the production of both goods A and B. Foreign is competitive in good B through F. At $\frac{w}{w*} = 12$, the cost of producing good B is the same in both Home and Foreign. Since both are competitive in good B, again there is indeterminacy in the production of good B, and hence the relative demand for Home labor has a horizontal segment at $\frac{w}{w*} = 12$. This pattern of horizontal segment and downward sloping segment continues as shown in Figure 2.5 till the relative wage hits 2 at which Foreign can compete only in good F. At this relative wage, Foreign can produce all of good F or no good F, and therefore the demand for Foreign labor can be as low as zero. This implies that the horizontal segment at $\frac{w}{w*} = 2$ extends to infinity.

The intersection of the relative demand and relative supply of labor determines the relative wage, which in turn determines the pattern of comparative advantage. For example, if the relative supply is given by RS_{I}, then the equilibrium relative wage is 11, and hence Home has a comparative advantage in goods A and B and Foreign has a comparative advantage in goods C, D, E and F. If the relative supply curve is given by RS_{II}, then the equilibrium relative wage is eight and now Home has a comparative advantage in A, B and C and Foreign in E and F. Both countries are equally good at producing D.

In general, given the numbers in Table 2.2, the equilibrium relative wage will settle in the range $\frac{w}{w*} \in [2, 15]$. Furthermore, both countries will gain from trade as long as it is cheaper to import some good which will be the case except at the two extremes: $\frac{w}{w*} = 2$ or $\frac{w}{w*} = 15$. In the former case, Foreign does not have a comparative advantage in any good. Home has a comparative advantage in A, B, C, D and E, and both are equally good at making F. Therefore, Home does not gain from trade in this case. In the latter case of $\frac{w}{w*} = 15$, Foreign has a comparative advantage in B, C, D, E, and F, and both are equally good at making A. Therefore, Foreign does not gain from trade in this case. In a world with many countries and many goods, all countries will gain from trade because it is virtually impossible for a country to be the least cost producer of all goods.

2.5.1 *Transportation cost*

So far, we have been assuming costless trade. That is, shipping goods across countries does not cost anything. However, the multi-goods Ricardian model discussed earlier can easily incorporate transport cost. The implication of introducing transportation cost is that some of the goods may be rendered non-traded. That is, these goods are produced and consumed domestically and not traded internationally. To see this, suppose that in the absence of transportation costs, the equilibrium is the one in Figure 2.5 when the relative supply curve is $\mathrm{RS}_{\mathrm{II}}$ so that Home has a comparative advantage in A, B and C and Foreign in E and F. Both are equally good at producing D. This implies that $p_i < p_i^*$ for $i = A, B, C, p_i < p_i^*$ for $i = E, F$ and $p_D = p_D^*$. Now, suppose that there is a per unit transportation cost of t of shipping goods across borders. What it means is that the price of good i shipped from Home to Foreign will be $p_i + t$. Similarly, price of good-i shipped from Foreign to Home will be $p_i^* + t$. Clearly, now good D will become non-tradable because $p_D < p_D^* + t$ and $p_D + t > p_D^*$. It is also possible for some other goods such as C or E to become non-tradable. We know that $p_C < p_C^*$ because Home has a comparative advantage in C, but it is possible that $p_C + t > p_C^*$ now so that good C becomes non-tradable.

2.6 Empirical Evidence on the Ricardian Model

The first empirical test of the Ricardian model was undertaken by a British economist named Robert MacDougall using from data 1937 from the US and the UK.[3] He collected data on labor productivity and trade for 26 manufacturing industries in the two countries. MacDougall wanted to test the following implication of the Ricardian model: *A country exports goods with higher ratios of productivity to wage and imports goods with lower ratios of productivity to wage.* This simply is another way of stating the condition $\frac{w}{w*} < \frac{a^*_{Li}}{a_{Li}}$ that we derived earlier. As mentioned earlier, productivity is the inverse of unit labor requirement. Let us use the notations $\mu_{Li}\frac{1}{a_{Li}}$ and $\mu^*_{Li} = \frac{1}{a^*_{Li}}$ to denote labor productivity in Home and Foreign, respectively. Then, the comparative advantage condition $\frac{w}{w*} < \frac{a^*_{Li}}{a_{Li}}$ can be rewritten as $\frac{\mu_{Li}}{w} > \frac{\mu^*_{Li}}{w^*}$. This simply states that Home has a comparative advantage in good-i if Home's productivity relative to wage is higher in good-i than that of Foreign.

Instead of looking at the export of the US to Britain and vice versa, MacDougall looked at the export of these countries to third markets such as Japan and France. The reason is that each country may be protecting its own market, which will distort the trade pattern, but they compete on equal footing in third markets. Then, MacDougall plotted the ratio of the US exports to the British exports against the ratio of the US productivity to the British productivity. What he found was that the US exports exceeded the British exports in industries where the US productivity was more than twice the British productivity and the opposite was true in industries where the US productivity was less than twice the British productivity. Can this be construed as supportive of the Ricardian model? The answer is yes due to the following reason. The US had an absolute advantage in all industries: US productivity was higher than British

[3]MacDougall, G. (1951). British and American Exports: A study suggested by the theory of comparative costs. Part I. *The Economic Journal, 61*(244): 697–724.

productivity and the productivity advantage ranged from 11% to 366%. Therefore, if trade was based on absolute productivity, then the US should have had a comparative advantage in all industries. However, the US wage was roughly twice the British wage, which meant that the US would have a comparative advantage in only those industries where its productivity was more than twice the British productivity. Therefore, the data were roughly consistent with the prediction of the Ricardian model.

It is worth pointing out that if the US has a comparative advantage in an industry, then according to the strict interpretation of the Ricardian model, the US should be the only exporter in that industry, and hence the ratio of the US to British exports should be infinite. Similarly, if Britain has a comparative advantage in an industry, then Britain should be the sole exporter, and hence the ratio of the US to British exports should be zero in that industry. However, MacDougall did not find any zero or infinite ratio. In fact, he was looking at whether the ratio exceeded one or was below one. There are a couple of reasons why MacDougall did not expect to find the extreme ratios of zero or infinity. First, these 26 industries are at a high level of aggregation and each contains a large number of products. Therefore, it is possible that the US has a comparative advantage in chemicals overall, but Britain has a comparative advantage in certain types of chemicals. Second, transportation costs can give a country a relative advantage in exporting goods to a destination closer to the origin. For example, the US may have a comparative advantage in apparels, but after including transportation cost, it may be cheaper for France to import apparels from Britain than the US.

Later, empirical tests of the Ricardian model confirmed the importance of relative productivity differences in determining the pattern of comparative advantage.

2.7 Concluding Remarks

We looked at two versions of the Ricardian model. A two-good, two-country model and a many-goods, two-country model. More recently, economists have developed versions of the Ricardian model with many countries and many goods. This version of the model has been very successful in capturing the pattern of trade among countries and is also very useful in providing numerical estimates of the gains from trade or the losses from trade barriers.

Before concluding this chapter, it is worth pointing out that an important assumption underlying the Ricardian model is the perfect mobility of labor within a country. This assumption is also crucial in deriving the result that potentially everyone can gain from trade. That is, we assumed that workers can costlessly move from the import-competing sector to the export sector after opening up to trade. In reality, it may be costly for workers to move. To the extent that it is costly for workers to move, the gains from trade are reduced.

Problem Set

Question 1

Suppose the unit labor requirements in Home and Foreign for the two goods Cloth and Wheat are as follows.

Unit Labor Requirements		
	Cloth	Wheat
Home	30	20
Foreign	60	30

Answer the following multiple choice questions based on the table above.

a) Given the information in the table above, Home has an absolute advantage in

   A) Cloth
   B) Wheat
   C) Both Cloth and Wheat
   D) Neither

b) Given the information in the table above, the opportunity cost of Cloth in Home is

A) 1 Wheat
B) 2 Wheat
C) 1.5 Wheat
D) 4 Wheat

c) Given the information in the table above, the opportunity cost of Wheat in Foreign is

A) 1 Cloth
B) 2 Cloths
C) ½Cloth
D) 4 Cloths

d) Given the information in the table above, the relative price of Cloth (Price of Cloth/Price of Wheat) in Home in autarky is going to be

A) 1
B) 2
C) 1.5
D) 4

e) Which of the following statements is true about the table above?

A) Home has a lower labor productivity in both Cloth and Wheat.
B) Foreign has a lower labor productivity in both Cloth and Wheat.
C) Home has a higher labor productivity in cloth, but Foreign has a higher labor productivity in Wheat.
D) Home has a lower labor productivity in cloth, but Foreign has a higher labor productivity in Wheat.

f) Which of the following statements is true about the table above?

A) Home has a comparative advantage in both Cloth and Wheat.
B) Foreign has a comparative advantage in both Cloth and Wheat.
C) Home has a comparative advantage in Cloth and Foreign in Wheat
D) Foreign has a comparative advantage in Cloth and Home in Wheat.

Question 2

Below are five examples of unit labor requirements for a foreign country (denoted with an asterisk) and a home country. There are two goods: good-1 and good-2. For each example, show which country has the comparative advantage in which good, and which country has the absolute advantage.

(a)	$a_{L1} = 0.5$	$a_{L2} = 0.2$	$a^*_{L1} = 0.2$	$a^*_{L2} = 0.5$
(b)	$a_{L1} = 0.5$	$a_{L2} = 0.2$	$a^*_{L1} = 0.25$	$a^*_{L2} = 0.1$
(c)	$a_{L1} = 0.6$	$a_{L2} = 0.3$	$a^*_{L1} = 0.1$	$a^*_{L2} = 0.3$
(d)	$a_{L1} = 0.7$	$a_{L2} = 0.1$	$a^*_{L1} = 0.7$	$a^*_{L2} = 0.07$
(e)	$a_{L1} = 0.4$	$a_{L2} = 0.1$	$a^*_{L1} = 0.004$	$a^*_{L2} = 0.002$

Question 3

Assume that there are two countries, Thailand and Vietnam, and two goods, rice and scooters. Unit labor requirements, a_{Li} (for Thailand) and a^*_{Li} (for Vietnam) and the labor force, L (in Thailand) and L^* (in Vietnam) are given below.

$$a_{LS} = 1.00 \quad a^*_{LS} = 0.50$$
$$a_{LR} = 0.20 \quad a^*_{LR} = 0.05$$
$$L = 200 \quad L^* = 100$$

(a) Draw the production possibility frontiers (PPFs) for Thailand and Vietnam, with scooters on the horizontal axis. Label your graphs carefully.

(b) Assume that the post-trade relative price of scooters in terms of rice, P^W_S/P^W_R, equals 7.5. Set the price of rice equal to one (i.e., choose rice as the numeraire good). Furthermore, assume that each country wishes to consume 100 scooters. Indicate the amounts produced, consumed, exported, imported, and the value of exports and imports for Thailand and Vietnam. Enter your results in a table with columns for each country and rows for the required information.

(c) Verify that trade in this example is <u>feasible</u> (one country's exports are another country's imports) and <u>balanced</u> (value of exports equals value of imports for each country).

Question 4

Consider the following Ricardian example with many goods, using standard Ricardian assumptions. There are two countries: Argentina and Chile. The unit labor requirements for Argentina are denoted by a_{Li} and for Chile by a^*_{Li}

	a_{Li}	a^*_{Li}
Cars	100	400
Laptops	50	150
Soybeans	25	50
Pharmaceuticals	20	30
Apparels	15	10

a) Clearly state which country has an absolute advantage in each of the 5 goods.

b) What condition determines if a country has a comparative advantage in a good?

c) Now, suppose the wage in Argentina $w = 15$ and the wage in Chile $w^* = 10$. Which goods does Argentina have a comparative advantage in? Which goods does Chile have a comparative advantage in?

d) What if the wage in Argentina $w = 25$ and the wage in Chile $w^* = 10$? Which goods does Argentina have a comparative advantage in? Which goods does Chile have a comparative advantage in?

e) Assume that the wage is the same as in part (d). Suppose that transportation costs were 20% of production costs (note that the production cost here is simply the labor cost). Will this lead to any good becoming a non-traded good?

f) Assume that the wage is the same as in part (d). Suppose that transportation costs were 100% of production costs. Will this lead to any good becoming a non-traded good?

Chapter 3

The Heckscher–Ohlin Model

3.1 Introduction

Named after two Swedish economists, Eli Heckscher and Bertil Ohlin, the Heckscher–Ohlin model studies the pattern of production and trade that arises when countries have different endowments of factors of production, such as labor, capital and land. It is also called factor proportions theory because it emphasizes the interplay between the proportions in which different factors are available in different countries and in which they are used in the production of different goods. In contrast to the Ricardian model where the pattern of comparative advantage, and consequently the pattern of trade, is determined by technological differences, in the Heckscher–Ohlin model, it is determined by the differences in the availability of different factors of production.

While writing in the early 20th century, Heckscher and Ohlin observed a large volume of trade between the US and Europe during the period 1870–1913. The pattern of trade was one where the US was exporting mainly agricultural goods, whereas Europe was exporting mainly manufacturing. This pattern of trade was not easy to explain according to the Ricardian model because it was hard to make the case that the US had a superior technology to produce agriculture and Europe had a superior technology to produce manufacturing. What was true though was that the US had a lot of land and fewer workers per unit of land, while Europe had a lot of workers per unit of land. Could the abundance of land in the US give it a comparative advantage in agriculture? This is the question that Heckscher and Ohlin answered using their model. An additional motivation for studying this model is that since the model has more than one factor of production, it shows the possibility that trade can produce winners and losers. Even though the original Heckscher–Ohlin model is in terms of land and labor, we discuss this model using a different example.

We first discuss a $2 \times 2 \times 2$ model with 2 countries, 2 goods and 2 factors of production and later discuss how it can be generalized to many goods, many factors and many countries. Suppose that the two countries are Home and Foreign, the two goods are Apparels and Computers and the two factors of production are labor and capital. The model is based on several assumptions which we discuss below.

3.2 Key Assumptions

The two countries differ with respect to the endowments of the two factors of production. We assume that Home is relatively abundant in capital and Foreign is relatively abundant in labor. Denote the amounts of capital and labor in country-j by K^j, L^j, respectively, where $j = \mathrm{H}, \mathrm{F}$. The factor endowment assumption implies that

$$\frac{K^{\mathrm{H}}}{L^{\mathrm{H}}} > \frac{K^{\mathrm{F}}}{L^{\mathrm{F}}}.$$

In fact, this is the only dimension along which the two countries differ. Everything else is identical between the two countries.

The technology for producing Apparels and Computers is exactly the same in the two countries. Both goods use both factors of production, and the production functions exhibit constant returns to scale. More importantly, one of the two goods is more capital intensive than the other. This is called the *factor intensity assumption.* We assume that Computers are more capital intensive than Apparels. What this means is that the capital–labor ratio used in the Computer production is always greater than the capital–labor ratio in the

Apparel production. If we denote the amount of capital used in good-i by K_i and the amount of labor used by L_i, then

$$\frac{K_{\mathrm{C}}}{L_{\mathrm{C}}} > \frac{K_{\mathrm{A}}}{L_{\mathrm{A}}},$$

where subscript C is for Computers and A is for Apparels. This is one of the key assumptions of the HO model, as will become clear later. To make this assumption concrete, let us assume the following production functions for the two goods:

$$Q_{\mathrm{C}} = A_{\mathrm{C}} K_{\mathrm{C}}^{\gamma} L_{\mathrm{C}}^{1-\gamma}, \tag{3.1}$$

$$Q_{\mathrm{A}} = A_{\mathrm{A}} K_{\mathrm{A}}^{\delta} L_{\mathrm{A}}^{1-\delta}. \tag{3.2}$$

In the above Cobb–Douglas production functions, A_i is a constant term and γ and δ are the parameters that determine the share of each factor (capital and labor) in total cost. We assume that $\gamma > \delta$ which will ensure that $\frac{K_{\mathrm{C}}}{L_{\mathrm{C}}} > \frac{K_{\mathrm{A}}}{L_{\mathrm{A}}}$ for any prices of labor and capital. If either labor or capital becomes cheaper, then firms hire more of the cheaper factor to minimize their costs. The factor intensity assumption ensures that the ratio of capital to labor is always higher in Computer production than Apparel production.

The remaining assumptions of the model are the same as those in the Ricardian model: Factors are freely mobile within a country but cannot move internationally; all goods and factor markets are perfectly competitive; preferences and hence relative demand for the two goods are identical in both countries; there are no barriers to trade in goods.

Having enlisted the assumptions of the model, we derive the autarky in a country first and then derive the trading equilibrium. In the process of deriving autarky equilibrium, we also derive a couple of very important results.

3.3 Autarky Equilibrium

Let us first derive the autarky equilibrium in Home. We derive the relative supply curve of Computers in Home and then bring in the downward sloping relative demand curve to determine the relative price of Computers in the autarky equilibrium.

The first step is to derive the relative supply curve of Computers as a function of the relative price of Computers. Denote the nominal price of Computers by P_{C} and the nominal price of Apparels by P_{A}. The relative price of Computers is $\frac{P_{\mathrm{C}}}{P_{\mathrm{A}}}$. Let us start with $\frac{P_{\mathrm{C}}}{P_{\mathrm{A}}} = 10$. This means that the price of a Computer is 10 times the price of an Apparel. Alternatively, one Computer is exchanged for 10 Apparels. Using our production function given earlier, we are going to draw an isoquant for 1 Computer and an isoquant for 10 Apparels. The isoquants are a representation of production function in the input space. The two inputs here are capital and labor. Therefore, we will draw the isoquants in the (labor, capital) space with labor on the horizontal axis and capital on the vertical axis. The isoquant for one unit of Computer gives all possible combinations of capital and labor that can be used to produce one Computer. The isoquant is going to be downward sloping and convex to the origin, given the production function above. We can similarly draw an isoquant corresponding to 10 Apparels. Given our factor intensity assumption (Computers are more capital intensive than Apparels), it will be the case that the isoquant for Apparels lies below the isoquant for Computers and they will intersect only once. Figure 3.1 draws isoquants corresponding to $Q_{\mathrm{C}} = 1$ and $Q_{\mathrm{A}} = 10$.

Having drawn the isoquants which capture various combinations of capital and labor that can be used to produce 1 Computer or 10 Apparels, we want to find out which combination of capital and labor firms will actually use. The goal of firms is to minimize the cost of production, so they will choose the combination that minimizes the cost. To determine this, we need information on the wage of labor and the rental of capital. Let us denote the wage by w and the rental of capital by r. Since factor markets are competitive, firms will take the factor prices as given and minimize their costs. Therefore, the Computer-producing firm is performing the following cost minimization exercise:

$$\underset{L_{\mathrm{C}},K_{\mathrm{C}}}{\mathrm{Min}} \{wL_{\mathrm{C}} + rK_{\mathrm{C}}\} \quad \text{s.t. } A_{\mathrm{C}}K_{\mathrm{C}}^{\gamma}L_{\mathrm{C}}^{1-\gamma} = 1.$$

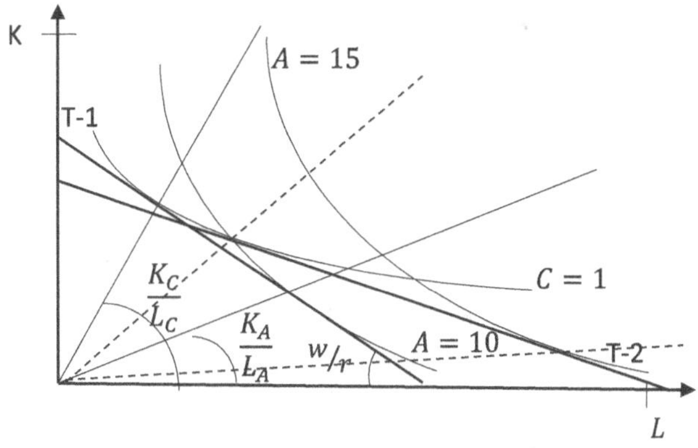

Figure 3.1: Lerner's diagram.

That is, the firm wants to choose the cost-minimizing combination of (L_C, K_C) to produce 1 Computer. Similarly, the Apparel firm performs the following cost minimization exercise to produce 10 units of Apparels:

$$\underset{L_A K_A}{\text{Min}} \{wL_A + rK_A\} \quad \text{s.t.} \ A_A K_A^{\delta} L_A^{1-\delta} = 10.$$

The standard cost minimization exercise works as follows. Given the factor prices, w and r, an isocost line can be defined as all combinations of capital and labor that result in a particular value of total cost. For example, one can set the total cost to 30 and draw an isocost line corresponding to $wL_A + rK_A = 30$. This isocost line is going to be a negatively sloped straight line in the (L, K) space with the absolute value of the slope equaling $\frac{w}{r}$. The firm's cost minimization exercise involves first drawing the isoquant corresponding to the value of output that it wants to produce and then drawing a family of parallel isocost lines with the slope $\frac{w}{r}$ and finding the isocost line closest to the origin that touches the isoquant. This is going to be given by an isocost line that is tangent to the isoquant. The point of tangency gives the optimal combination of (L, K) to produce that level of output for a given factor price.

In our case here, we do not know the factor prices. In fact, one of our goals is to find the factor prices corresponding to the product price ratio of 10. This can be found by asking the following question. What level of factor prices will allow both Computers and Apparels to be produced in Home in such a way that one Computer is exchanged for 10 Apparels? Since all markets are perfectly competitive, if the price of a Computer is 10 times the price of an Apparel, the cost of producing a Computer should also be 10 times the cost of producing an Apparel. Diagrammatically, the cost of producing one Computer equals the cost of producing 10 Apparels if the same isocost line is tangent to the isoquant for 1 Computer and the isoquant for 10 Apparels. As shown in Figure 3.1, we draw a common tangent, the solid line denoted by T-1, to the unit isoquants and claim that the factor price ratio $\frac{w}{r}$ corresponding to $\frac{P_{\mathrm{C}}}{P_{\mathrm{A}}} = 10$ should be given by the slope of this common isocost line. It can be verified that if the $\frac{w}{r}$ ratio is anything else, then the isocost line tangent to the Computer isoquant lies either to the left or to the right of the isocost line tangent to the Apparels isoquant. Therefore, either the cost of producing one Computer is greater than the cost of producing 10 Apparels, in which case it is unprofitable to produce Computers, or the cost of producing one Computer is less than the cost of producing 10 Apparels, in which case only Apparels will be produced. Therefore, for both goods to be produced at $\frac{P_{\mathrm{C}}}{P_{\mathrm{A}}} = 10$, the factor price ratio, $\frac{w}{r}$, must correspond to the slope of the common tangent in Figure 3.1.

Next, the points of tangency between the isoquants and the common isoquant line in Figure 3.1 also give us the optimal combination of (L_{C}, K_{C}) to produce 1 Computer and the optimal combination of $(L_{\mathrm{A}}, K_{\mathrm{A}})$ to produce 10 Apparels. The slopes of the rays from the origin to these points of tangency are given by $\frac{K_{\mathrm{C}}}{L_{\mathrm{C}}}$ and $\frac{K_{\mathrm{A}}}{L_{\mathrm{A}}}$ (verify that as $\frac{K_{\mathrm{C}}}{L_{\mathrm{C}}} > \frac{K_{\mathrm{A}}}{L_{\mathrm{A}}}$ required by our factor intensity assumption). Using these factor intensity ratios and the total amount of capital and labor in Home, we can find the amounts of Computers and Apparels produced at $\frac{P_{\mathrm{C}}}{P_{\mathrm{A}}} = 10$. We will do this both algebraically and diagrammatically. Let us first do it algebraically.

Algebraically,

$$K_{\mathrm{C}} + K_{\mathrm{A}} = K^{\mathrm{H}}.$$

Next, divide both sides by L^{H} to obtain

$$\frac{K_{\mathrm{C}}}{L^{\mathrm{H}}} + \frac{K_{\mathrm{A}}}{L^{\mathrm{H}}} = \frac{K^{\mathrm{H}}}{L^{\mathrm{H}}}.$$

Next, multiply and divide the first term on the left-hand side by L_{C} and the second term by L_{A} to obtain

$$\frac{L_{\mathrm{C}}}{L_{\mathrm{C}}}\frac{K_{\mathrm{C}}}{L^{\mathrm{H}}} + \frac{L_{\mathrm{A}}}{L_{\mathrm{A}}}\frac{K_{\mathrm{A}}}{L^{\mathrm{H}}} = \frac{K^{\mathrm{H}}}{L^{\mathrm{H}}}.$$

Rearrange the left-hand side to obtain

$$\frac{L_{\mathrm{C}}}{L^{\mathrm{H}}}\frac{K_{\mathrm{C}}}{L_{\mathrm{C}}} + \frac{L_{\mathrm{A}}}{L^{\mathrm{H}}}\frac{K_{\mathrm{A}}}{L_{\mathrm{A}}} = \frac{K^{\mathrm{H}}}{L^{\mathrm{H}}}.$$

Finally, rewrite the above as

$$\lambda\frac{K_{\mathrm{C}}}{L_{\mathrm{C}}} + (1-\lambda)\frac{K_{\mathrm{A}}}{L_{\mathrm{A}}} = \frac{K^{\mathrm{H}}}{L^{\mathrm{H}}},$$

where $\lambda \equiv \frac{L_{\mathrm{C}}}{L^{\mathrm{H}}}$.

Note from the above equation that since we know $\frac{K_{\mathrm{C}}}{L_{\mathrm{C}}}$ and $\frac{K_{\mathrm{A}}}{L_{\mathrm{A}}}$ from Figure 3.1 and $\frac{K^{\mathrm{H}}}{L^{\mathrm{H}}}$ is given, the above is an equation in one unknown λ. The value of λ is given by

$$\lambda = \frac{\frac{K^{\mathrm{H}}}{L^{\mathrm{H}}} - \frac{K_{\mathrm{A}}}{L_{\mathrm{A}}}}{\frac{K_{\mathrm{C}}}{L_{\mathrm{C}}} - \frac{K_{\mathrm{A}}}{L_{\mathrm{A}}}}. \tag{3.3}$$

Once we know λ, we know L_{C}, and hence $L_{\mathrm{A}}(= L^{\mathrm{H}} - L_{\mathrm{C}})$. Since we already know $\frac{K_{\mathrm{C}}}{L_{\mathrm{C}}}$ and $\frac{K_{\mathrm{A}}}{L_{\mathrm{A}}}$, the knowledge of L_{C} and L_{A} yields K_{C} and K_{A}. Therefore, we basically know how much capital and labor goes into Computer production and how much into Apparel production. From the production function given in Equations (3.1) and (3.2), this immediately gives the amounts of Computers and Apparels produced. The ratio of Computers to Apparels produced is one point on our relative supply curve corresponding to a relative price of $\frac{P_{\mathrm{C}}}{P_{\mathrm{A}}} = 10$.

To find out the amounts of capital and labor going into Computers and Apparel production diagrammatically, draw a rectangular

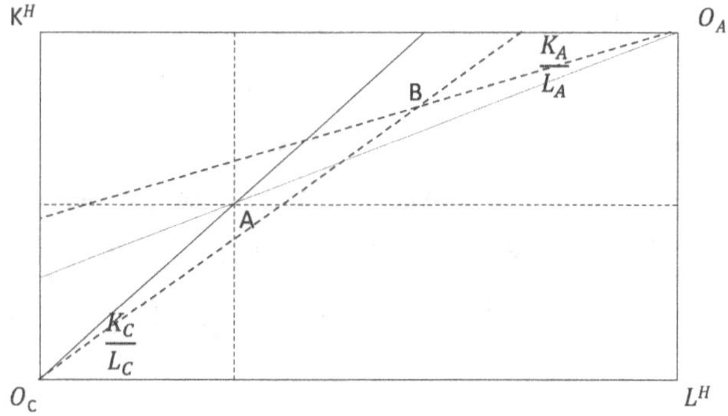

Figure 3.2: Endowment box.

box with the horizontal dimension equal to the amount of labor in Home, L^{H}, and the vertical dimension equal to the amount of capital in Home, K^{H}, as shown in Figure 3.2.

Next, using the southwest origin as the Computer origin, O_{C}, draw a line with slope $\frac{K_{\mathrm{C}}}{L_{\mathrm{C}}}$. Similarly, using the northeast origin as the Apparel origin, O_{A}, draw a line with slope $\frac{K_{\mathrm{A}}}{L_{\mathrm{A}}}$. Verify that the intersection of the two lines gives the allocation of capital and labor between Computers and Apparels production. The coordinates of the point of intersection, A, measured from the origin O_{C} give the amount of labor and capital used in Computers and the coordinates measured from the origin O_{A} give the amount of labor and capital used in Apparels.

Let us recap what we have done so far. We started with a relative price of Computers of 10 and then we determined the ratio corresponding to this price, which in turn gave us the capital–labor ratio used in the two goods which allowed us to derive the amounts of capital and labor going into the production of each good and consequently the quantity of each good produced. While we determined $\frac{w}{r}$ ratio we have not said anything about the determination of real rewards of the two factors of production. The real rewards are expressed in terms of the goods consumed as was mentioned in the discussion of the Ricardian model. Therefore, the real reward of labor is $\frac{w}{P_{\mathrm{C}}}$ and $\frac{w}{P_{\mathrm{A}}}$ in terms of Computers and Apparels, respectively. Similarly, the real reward of capital is $\frac{r}{P_{\mathrm{C}}}$ and

$\frac{r}{P_A}$ in terms of Computers and Apparels, respectively. We already have enough information to determine these real rewards when the relative price of Computers is 10. The real rewards can be obtained as follows. Recall our assumption of all goods and factor markets being perfectly competitive. What this means is that the factor rewards are going to be equated to the value of marginal products. To fix ideas, let us look at the labor market and the behavior of Computer-producing firms. If the wage is w, how do firms decide how many workers to hire? A Computer-producing firm keeps hiring workers till the extra revenue that it gets by hiring an additional worker exceeds w. The extra revenue from hiring an additional worker is simply the price of Computers multiplied by the marginal product of that worker: $P_C \times \text{MPL}_C$. Hence, the real wage in terms of Computers $\frac{w}{P_C} = \text{MPL}_C$.

Given the production function in Equations (3.1) and (3.2), it is easy to verify that the marginal product of a worker in Computer production is

$$\text{MPL}_C \equiv \frac{\partial Q_C}{\partial L_C} = (1-\gamma)A_C K_C^{\gamma} L_C^{-\gamma} = (1-\gamma)A_C \left(\frac{K_C}{L_C}\right)^{\gamma}.$$

The last equality above says that the marginal product of labor in Computer production is simply a function of the capital–labor ratio used in Computer production. This convenient feature of the constant returns to scale production function implies that the real wage in terms of Computers is simply an increasing function of the capital–labor ratio used in Computer production. Using the same steps, we can write the real rewards of both factors of production in terms of Computers and Apparels as follows.

$$\frac{w}{P_C} = (1-\gamma)A_C \left(\frac{K_C}{L_C}\right)^{\gamma}; \quad \frac{w}{P_A} = (1-\delta)A_A \left(\frac{K_A}{L_A}\right)^{\delta}, \tag{3.4}$$

$$\frac{r}{P_C} = rA_C \left(\frac{K_C}{L_C}\right)^{\gamma-1}; \quad \frac{r}{P_A} = \delta A_A \left(\frac{K_A}{L_A}\right)^{\delta-1}. \tag{3.5}$$

Now that we have derived all variables of interest corresponding to the relative price of 10, we change the relative price and see what happens. Suppose that the relative price of Computers increases to 15. It immediately implies that 1 Computer is exchanged for 15 Apparels now. Therefore, to capture this new price ratio, in Figure 3.1 we have to draw an isoquant for Apparels corresponding to 15 units. This must lie to the right of the isoquant for 10 units of Apparels. Next, draw the common tangent to the two isoquants capturing the relative price of 15. The common tangent in Figure 3.1 is the solid line denoted by T-2. Note that the common tangent is flatter than before: Line T-2 is flatter than line T-1. Since the slope of the common tangent is $\frac{w}{r}$, what this means is that an increase in the relative price of Computers lowers the $\frac{w}{r}$ ratio. From the new points of tangencies, also verify that the capital–labor ratios used in both Computers and Apparels production go down (dashed rays from the origin). This make sense because if labor becomes cheaper relative to capital, firms should use more labor and less capital to minimize their cost of production. Use these new capital–labor ratios in Figure 3.2 to find the new allocation of capital and labor between Computers and Apparels. The new capital–labor ratios in the two sectors are depicted by dashed lines in Figure 3.2. Verify from Figure 3.2 that the new intersection of the capital–labor ratio lines at point B implies that more labor and capital go into Computer production leaving less for Apparels production. Therefore, the amount of Computers produced increases and the amount of Apparels produced decreases. In other words, when the relative price of Computers increases, the relative supply of Computers increases. Thus, we have derived an upward sloping relative supply curve which is drawn in Figure 3.3.

The intersection of this upward sloping relative supply curve with the downward sloping relative demand curve yields the autarky equilibrium relative price in Home. This is denoted by $(\frac{P_C}{P_A})^H$ in Figure 3.3.

Before determining the pattern of trade, we derive an important result on the relationship between goods prices and factor prices. This result is known as the *Stolper–Samuelson Theorem*.[1] The statement of the theorem is as follows.

---

[1]Stolper, W. and Samuelson, P. (1941). Protection and real wages. *The Review of Economic Studies*, *9*(1): 58–73.

Stolper–Samuelson Theorem. *Increasing the relative price of a good, holding factor supplies constant, increases the relative reward of the factor used intensively in the production of that good. Additionally, it also increases the real reward of that factor, while lowering the real return to the other factor.*

In the context of our model, the theorem says that an increase in the relative price of the capital-intensive good, Computers, will lead to an increase in the real reward of capital and a decrease in the real reward of labor. The proof of the theorem is straightforward. We have already established in Figure 3.1 that an increase in the relative price of Computers from 10 to 15 leads to a decrease in the capital labor ratio in both goods and an increase in the relative reward of capital. It follows from the expressions for real rewards in Equations (3.4) and (3.5) that a decrease in capital–labor ratio implies a decrease in the real wage and an increase in the real rental of capital.

The intuition behind this very important result can be understood in two different ways. One way to understand it is to note that since the relative price of Computers increases, firms should find it more profitable to produce Computers. Since Computers are more capital intensive, the relative demand for capital increases, increasing the relative price of capital. An alternative, and more mechanical, way to understand it is to note that if the relative price of Computers increases, given the perfectly competitive markets, the relative cost of producing Computers must increase as well. Now, this can happen

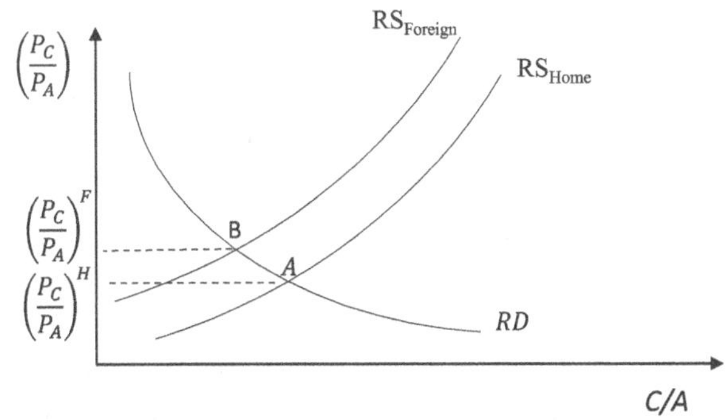

Figure 3.3: Relative demand, relative supply.

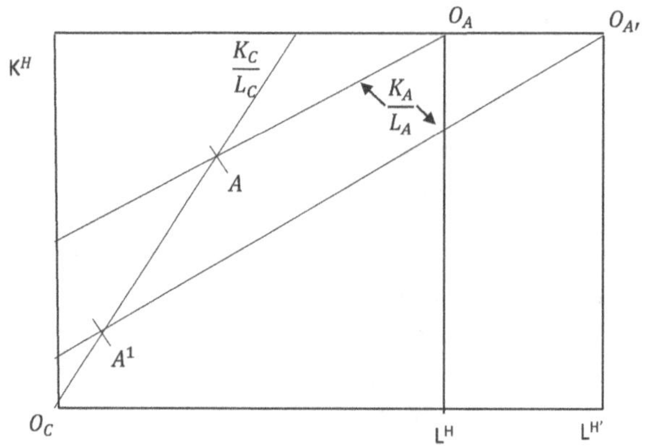

Figure 3.4: Increase in endowment.

only if the relative reward of capital increases because an increase in the relative reward of labor will increase the relative cost of producing the more labor-intensive good, which is Apparels.

Having determined the autarky equilibrium and verified the Stolper–Samuelson theorem, we now want to know the relative supply curve in Foreign which is relatively labor abundant. Recall from assumptions that the only difference between Home and Foreign is in terms of their factor endowments. Therefore, to derive Foreign's relative supply curve, we find out what would happen to the autarky equilibrium in Home if Home receives more labor holding the same amount of capital. This exercise will also help us establish an important result known as the Rybczynski theorem.

Now, if Home has more labor keeping the amount of capital the same, then Home's endowment box in Figure 3.2 will be stretched horizontally. Recall that the horizontal dimension of the box is the amount of Labor Home has. Therefore, the new box with more labor will be longer but with the same height as shown in Figure 3.4. A consequence is that the new origin for Apparels is given by $O^{A'}$.

Now, let us determine the amount of Computers and Apparels produced in Home at the relative price of 10 when Home has the larger endowment box. Since our determination of capital–labor ratio in Figure 3.1 was independent of the endowment of capital and labor for Home, these ratios do not change. Therefore, all we have to do is plot the same capital–labor ratio for Apparels as in the original box but from the origin $O^{A\prime}$. Since the capital-labor ratio is unchanged, the capital–labor ratio line from $O^{A\prime}$ will be parallel to the one from O^{A}. The intersection of the capital–labor ratio line from $O^{A\prime}$ with the line from O^{C} gives the new allocation of capital and labor between Computers and Apparels. From the coordinates of the intersection point A', verify that more capital and labor go into Apparel production and less capital and labor go into Computer production. Therefore, there is an increase in the production of Apparels and a decrease in the production of Computers, and hence the relative supply of Computers goes down.

This result can be established algebraically as follows. Start with the expression for λ derived in Equation (3.3). Since we are doing the exercise at the relative price of 10, $\frac{K_C}{L_C}$ and $\frac{K_A}{L_A}$ are unchanged. Therefore, from Equation (3.3), we obtain

$$\frac{d\lambda}{d\left(\frac{K^H}{L^H}\right)} = \frac{1}{\frac{K_C}{L_C} - \frac{K_A}{L_A}} > 0.$$

That is, an increase in the capital–labor ratio in Home increases $\lambda(= \frac{L_C}{L^H})$, which is the share of labor going to Computer production. Note that we have increased L^H holding K^H constant in Figure 3.4. So, we have reduced $\frac{K^H}{L^H}$ in Figure 3.4. Therefore, it would lead to a decrease in λ, and hence an increase in $1 - \lambda = \frac{L_A}{L^H}$. An increase in $\frac{L_A}{L^H}$ must lead to an increase in L_A and consequently an increase K_A because $\frac{K_A}{L_A}$ is unchanged. Since the amount of K^H is unchanged, an increase in K_A must lead to a decrease in K_C, and hence a decrease in L_C because $\frac{K_C}{L_C}$ is unchanged. Therefore, we have verified the result we obtained diagrammatically that more capital and labor go into Apparel production and less into Computer production, and consequently the output of Computers decreases and the output of Apparels increases, leading to a decrease in the relative supply of Computers. This gives us a second important result known as the Rybczynski's theorem.[2]

[2]Rybczynski, T. (1955). Factor endowment and relative commodity prices. *Economica*, *22*(88): 336–341.

Rybczynski Theorem. *Increasing the relative supply of one factor, holding product prices constant, leads to a biased expansion of production possibilities favoring the relative supply of the good which uses that factor intensively.*

Now, we will use this result to derive the relative supply curve in Foreign. Recall our assumption that Home is relatively abundant in capital and Foreign is relatively abundant in labor: $\frac{K^{\mathrm{H}}}{L^{\mathrm{H}}} > \frac{K^{\mathrm{F}}}{L^{\mathrm{F}}}$. Given this, Rybczynski's theorem implies that at each relative price of Computers, the relative supply of Computers in Foreign is less than the relative supply in Home. That is, in Figure 3.3, the relative supply curve for Foreign lies to the left of the relative supply curve for Home. Since the relative demand curve in Foreign is the same as the relative demand curve in Home (given the assumption of identical preferences), the autarky equilibrium relative price in Foreign, denoted by $\left(\frac{P_{\mathrm{C}}}{P_{\mathrm{A}}}\right)^{\mathrm{F}}$ in Figure 3.3, is higher than that in Home. Therefore, Home has a comparative advantage in Computers and Foreign has a comparative advantage in Apparels. This gives us our key result of this chapter which is known as the Heckscher–Ohlin theorem and is described below.

Heckscher–Ohlin Theorem. *A country has a comparative advantage in the good that is relatively intensive in the country's relatively abundant factor.*

In our example, capital is the relatively abundant factor in Home, and hence Home has a comparative advantage in Computers which is the capital-intensive good. Similarly, Foreign is relatively abundant in labor, and hence Foreign has a comparative advantage in Apparels which is the labor-intensive good. It is worth reiterating that the only difference between the two countries in this model is in the relative endowment of the two factors of production, which forms the basis of comparative advantage and the pattern of trade.

Having determined the pattern of comparative advantage, we can also derive the world relative price of Computers, $\left(\frac{P_{\mathrm{C}}}{P_{\mathrm{A}}}\right)^{\mathrm{W}}$, at which the two countries will exchange goods. The world relative price of Computers is determined in a fashion identical to that in the Ricardian model discussed in Chapter 2. That is, the world relative price is determined by the world relative demand (which is the same as the relative demand in each country given the assumption of identical preferences) and the world relative supply. The world relative supply of Computers is a weighted average of the autarky relative supplies in the two countries, and hence lies between the two countries' relative supply curves. Therefore, the world relative price of Computers also lies between the autarky relative prices in Home and Foreign $\left(\frac{P_C}{P_A}\right)^H < \left(\frac{P_C}{P_A}\right)^W < \left(\frac{P_C}{P_A}\right)^F$.

3.4 Impact of Trade in the Heckscher–Ohlin Model

In the absence of transportation costs or other barriers to trade, international trade equalizes the relative prices of goods as was the case in the Ricardian model. The two countries exchange Computers and Apparels at the world relative price of $\left(\frac{P_C}{P_A}\right)^W$. Since the world relative price is different from the autarky price in each country, there are going to be aggregate gains from trade as in the Ricardian model. We will show the aggregate gains from trade subsequently, but we first discuss the impact of trade on factor prices.

3.4.1 *Impact on factor prices*

Unlike the Ricardian model where there was a single factor of production, the presence of two factors in the Heckscher–Ohlin model creates the possibility of winners and losers from trade. To see the impact of trade on factor prices, we are going to use the Stolper–Samuelson theorem derived earlier. International trade in our setting increases the relative price of Computers in Home, $\left(\frac{P_C}{P_A}\right)^H < \left(\frac{P_C}{P_A}\right)^W$, and reduces the relative price of Computers in Foreign, $\left(\frac{P_C}{P_A}\right)^W < \left(\frac{P_C}{P_A}\right)^F$. Therefore, we can conclude from the Stolper–Samuelson theorem that international trade increases the relative reward of capital in Home in addition to increasing the real reward of capital and decreasing the real reward of labor.

If capital owners are richer than workers, then the implication is that international trade increases inequality in the distribution of income in Home. Moreover, capital, owners gain from trade, but workers lose from trade. The opposite happens in Foreign. Here, international trade reduces the relative reward of capital, thereby reducing inequality. It also increases the real reward of labor and reduces the real reward of capital. Therefore, workers gain from trade in Foreign, but capital owners lose.

Another interesting result that comes out of the Heckscher–Ohlin model is the possibility of factor price equalization. That is, international trade equalizes not only the prices of goods which are traded but also the prices of factors of production which are not traded. The statement of the result is as follows.

Factor Price Equalization Theorem. *Trade in goods, which leads to the equalization of goods prices, can lead to an equalization in the real rewards of factors of production across countries.*

The theorem is easily proved using Figure 3.1. Since the goods prices are equalized after opening to trade, the world relative price of Computers can be captured by the same set of unit isoquants in both countries in Figure 3.1. Therefore, the line that is tangent to both the unit isoquants is identical in the two countries implying identical wage–rental ratios. This in turn implies identical capital–labor ratios in the two goods in both countries. It follows from the expressions for real rewards in Equations (3.4) and (3.5) that they are equalized.

Note that the statement of the theorem above uses “can” rather than “will” because the factor price equalization result is obtained only if both countries remain diversified, which means they keep producing both goods after opening up to trade. This would happen if the capital–labor ratios in the two countries are not too different.

The possibility of factor price equalization in the Heckscher–Ohlin model is a very powerful result because there is no movement of factors of production across borders. Trade in goods alone suffices to equalize the rewards of factors of production, thereby removing any incentive for factors of production to move across borders.

Having discussed the implications of trade for factor prices, we now turn to the question of aggregate gains from trade.

3.4.2 *Gains from trade*

The best way to illustrate the gains from trade in the Heckscher–Ohlin model is to use the production possibility frontier (PPF) and the indifference curve of a representative agent in the economy. We discussed the concept of PPF in Chapter 2 in the context of the Ricardian Model. The PPF for a country depicts all possible combinations of the two goods that a country can produce given its endowments of the factors of production and the technology to produce the two goods. In the Ricardian model, since there was a single factor of production, labor, and each good had a constant unit labor requirement, the opportunity cost of producing each good was constant, and hence the PPF was linear. That is, if a country wanted to produce one more unit of Cloth, it had to give up the same amount of Bread whether the country was producing a little Cloth or a lot of Cloth. In the present case with two factors of production, capital and labor, the PPF is going to be concave to the origin. That is, suppose that we depict Computers on the horizontal axis and Apparels on the vertical axis, then start at any point on the PPF (say $C = 100, A = 5000$) and say the country wants to produce one more Computer. It will have to withdraw capital and labor from Apparel production. The amounts of capital and labor that must be withdrawn capital and labor from Apparel production will determine how many Apparels the country has to give up to produce one more Computer. This in turn will determine the opportunity cost of a Computer. Suppose that it is 25. That is, to produce one more Computer, the country has to reduce Apparel production by 25. Therefore, we have another point on the PPF given by $C = 101$ and $A = 4975$. Now, if the country wants to produce one more Computer, the opportunity cost is likely to be greater than 25. The reason has to do with the fact that Apparel production is labor intensive while Computer production is capital intensive. When the production of Apparel is reduced, more labor and less capital are released, whereas Computer production requires more capital and less labor in relative

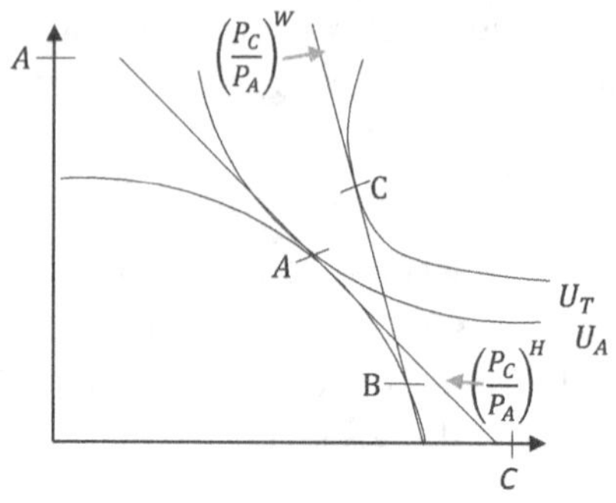

Figure 3.5: Welfare gains from trade.

terms. That is, the factors released by Apparel production are less suitable for Computer production and this unsuitability gets worse as more Computers and fewer Apparels are produced. The resulting PPF is shown in Figure 3.5.

A representative consumer's preferences for Computers and Apparels can be captured by downward sloping and convex indifference curves. The autarky equilibrium is shown by the tangency of the PPF with the highest possible indifference curve of the representative agent. This indifference curve is labeled u_{A} in Figure 3.5. The slope of the common tangent is the autarky relative price. Suppose that this is the country we called Home earlier. Therefore, the slope of the common tangent is $\left(\frac{P_{\mathrm{C}}}{P_{\mathrm{A}}}\right)^{\mathrm{H}}$. As discussed earlier, Home has a comparative advantage in Computers. As a result, when Home opens to trade, the world relative price of Computers is $\left(\frac{P_{\mathrm{C}}}{P_{\mathrm{A}}}\right)^{\mathrm{W}} > \left(\frac{P_{\mathrm{C}}}{P_{\mathrm{A}}}\right)^{\mathrm{H}}$. Thus, after opening up to trade, Home's producers and consumers face the relative price of $\left(\frac{P_{\mathrm{C}}}{P_{\mathrm{A}}}\right)^{\mathrm{W}}$. We can draw a relative price line with slope $\left(\frac{P_{\mathrm{C}}}{P_{\mathrm{A}}}\right)^{\mathrm{W}}$, which is tangent to PPF. This line is going to be steeper than the autarky common tangent whose slope is $\left(\frac{P_{\mathrm{C}}}{P_{\mathrm{A}}}\right)^{\mathrm{H}}$. When Home producers maximize their production facing a relative price of $\left(\frac{P_{\mathrm{C}}}{P_{\mathrm{A}}}\right)^{\mathrm{W}}$, the value of their production is maximized at the point of tangency, indicated by point B in Figure 3.5. Home consumers can consume anywhere on this line of tangency, which effectively becomes their budget constraint. They maximize their utility by choosing the highest possible indifference curve given the budget line passing through point B (the value of production) and the slope $\left(\frac{P_C}{P_A}\right)^W$. The point of tangency between the highest possible indifference curve, labeled u_T, and the budget line occurs at point C. Therefore, the country produces at point B and consumes at point C. Clearly, since point C lies to the northwest of point B, the country produces more Computers than it consumes and consumes more Apparels than it produces. Therefore, it exports Computers and imports Apparels. Note that the indifference curve labeled u_T lies to the right of the indifference curve labeled u_A. That is, the representative consumer experiences a higher level of utility after opening up to trade compared to autarky, meaning that the country gains from trade. The gains for Foreign can be illustrated in a similar fashion.

Next, we discuss some empirical evidence on various theoretical results derived in this chapter.

3.5 Empirical Evidence

3.5.1 *Historical evidence on factor price equalization*

Two economic historians Kevin O'Rourke and Jeffrey Williamson studied globalization during the period 1870–1913.[3] The pattern of trade during this period was one where land-abundant countries such as the US, Canada and Argentina were exporting agricultural products to Europe which was abundant in labor and the European countries were exporting manufacturing products. If one thinks of a model where the two factors of production are Land and Labor and the two goods are agriculture and manufacturing, and agriculture is land intensive while manufacturing is labor intensive, then the Heckscher–Ohlin model would predict that the labor abundant Europe would export manufacturing and the land-abundant countries would export agricultural products. Therefore, the pattern of trade was consistent with the Heckscher–Ohlin model. The factor

[3]Kevin H. O'Rourke and Williamson, J. G. (1999). Globalization and history: The evolution of a nineteenth century atlantic economy. MIT Press.

price prediction of such trade would be an increase in the relative reward of land in the land-abundant countries or a decrease in the relative reward of labor in those countries and the opposite in the labor-abundant countries. O'Rourke and Williamson found that the wage–rent ratio fell by half in the US, by three fourths in Australia, doubled in the UK and Sweden, and quintupled in Ireland. Therefore, the factor price changes were consistent with the Stolper–Samuelson predictions.

3.5.2 *Leontief paradox*

Wassily Leontief, a Nobel Prize-winning economist, conducted a more direct test of the Heckscher–Ohlin pattern of trade.[4] He hypothesized that since the US was the most capital-abundant country during his period of study which was right after the end of the Second World War, the US exports should be more capital intensive than the US imports. To test this idea, he constructed a representative basket of the US exports worth \$1 million and a representative basket of the US imports worth \$1 million. Next, using the input–output table for the US that he had constructed earlier, he backed out amount of capital and labor embodied in the representative export and import baskets and calculated the capital–labor ratio for each. What he found was that the capital–labor ratio in the representative basket of imports was higher than in the basket of exports. This is contrary to what he expected based on the Heckscher–Ohlin model, and hence the findings are known as the Leontief paradox. Several people ran this exercise in later years and confirmed Leontief's findings.

Some economists argued that the Leontief test was not the right test of Heckscher–Ohlin model. Later work on testing Heckscher–Ohlin model took a different approach, which is suitable for a multi-factor multi-country world. This approach is called the Heckscher–Ohlin–Vanek (HOV) approach, which we describe next.

---

[4]Leontief, W. (1953). Domestic production and foreign trade; the american capital position re-examined. *Proceedings of the American Philosophical Society, 97*(4): 332–349.

3.5.3 *Tests of HOV prediction*

The HOV prediction is based on the idea that trade in goods in the Heckscher–Ohlin world is an indirect way to trade factor services. That is, when a land-abundant country is exporting a land-intensive good like corn, it is indirectly exporting the services of land. The testable predictions are derived as follows. If a country's share in world GDP is 20%, then, assuming balanced trade, its share in world consumption must be 20% as well. Next, the assumption of identical preferences across countries implies that this country must consume 20% of all goods and services produced in the world. Next, if all countries use identical technologies to produce goods (an assumption of the HO model), then a country that consumes 20% of all goods produced in the world must consume 20% of the services of all factors of production in the world as well. However, a country does not own 20% of all factors of production in the world. Its share in some factors will exceed 20% and will be less than 20% in others. Suppose that this country owns 25% of the stock of world capital and 10% of the agricultural land. Then, according to the HOV prediction, this country should be a net exporter of the services of capital and a net importer of the services of land.

The first test of the HOV prediction was done by three economists Leamer, Bowen and Sveikauskas, published in a paper in the *American Economic Review* in 1987.[5] They looked at from data 1967 for 27 countries and 12 factors of production. For each factor of production in each country, using the data on endowments and the country's share in the world GDP, they obtained a measure of predicted factor content of trade. Then, using the trade data for the country and the input–output table for the US, they backed out the actual net factor content of trade for each factor of production. Then, they compared the predicted factor content of trade with the actual factor content of trade by performing a simple sign test: Does the actual factor content

[5]Bowen, H., Leamer, E., and Sveikauskas, L. (1987). Multicountry, multifactor tests of the factor abundance theory. *The American Economic Review*, 77(5): 791–809.

of trade have the same sign as the predicted factor content of trade? That is, if the prediction is that a country should be a net exporter of the services of capital, is that confirmed by the actual factor content of trade? The results were disappointing. The sign test passed in 61% of the cases, which is not too different from 50% (If there was no theory and things were completely random, one would expect the sign test to pass in 50% of the cases). In other words, their findings were not supportive of the Heckscher–Ohlin model.

The failure of the Heckscher–Ohlin model in trade data raises the following issue. We know that the model is logically correct, so if it doesn't find support in data, it must be because some of its assumptions are not realistic or do not apply in the real world. Further studies have attempted to understand which assumptions of the Heckscher–Ohlin model do not apply in the real world. An important study is that of Daniel Trefler, published in the American Economic Review in 1995.[6] Trefler used data from 1983 for 33 countries and 9 factors of production. He replicated the sign test of Leamer *et al.* (1987) and found that the sign test passed in only 50% of cases.

Digging deeper, Trefler also found that the measured (or actual) net factor content of trade was much smaller than the predicted factor content of trade, and in fact the former was very close to zero for a lot of countries and factors of production, a finding he dubbed as "missing trade". Trefler suspected that the assumption of identical technology was the main culprit. Both Leamer *et al.* and Trefler used the US input–output table to compute the measured factor content of trade. Now, if all countries have identical technologies and factor price equalization holds, then all countries' input–output tables must be the same. However, if technologies differ across countries, then this is not going to be so.

In an earlier paper published in the *Journal of Political Economy* in 1993,[7] Trefler had found evidence of productivity differences across countries which were reflected in factor price differences.

[6]Trefler, D. (1995). The case of the missing trade and other mysteries. *The American Economic Review*, *85*(5): 1029–1046.

[7]Trefler, D. (1993). International factor price differences: Leontief was right! *Journal of Political Economy*, *101*(6): 961–987.

For example, if a country's labor productivity was 10% of the US labor productivity, its wage was roughly 10% of the US wage. To account for differential productivity across countries, Trefler made some adjustments in the factor content calculation. This improved the sign test to 62%. He also allowed for Home bias in consumption (allowing countries to have a stronger preference for goods produced at Home rather than all countries having identical preferences), which improved the sign test to 72% of cases.

Trefler allowed the productivities of countries to differ by a scalar in which case factor prices will not be equalized in absolute terms but relative factor prices would be equalized and countries would continue to produce all goods. Another important study on this topic was conducted by two economists Donald Davis and David Weinstein, published in the American Economic Review in 2001.[8] In this study, they allowed the possibility of factor prices not being equalized even in relative terms. This was motivated by the fact that more capital-abundant countries tended to use higher capital intensity to produce a good than was the case in less capital-abundant country. That is, the capital–labor ratio in an industry tended to be positively correlated to the country's capital–labor ratio. They also relaxed the assumption of costless trade. They showed that making these adjustments significantly improves the empirical fit of the factor content model. That is, the modified HOV predictions find much stronger support in data than the "pure" Heckscher–Ohlin model. Therefore, even though there is weak support for the pure Heckscher–Ohlin model, a modified version that allows departure from factor price equalization due to significant endowment differences across countries and incorporates trade barriers performs much better in data.

3.6 Concluding Remarks

The Heckscher–Ohlin theorem is a very important result in international trade theory which links the pattern of comparative advantage and trade to endowment differences across countries. Even though

[8]Davis, D. R., and Weinstein, D. E. (2001). An account of global factor trade. *American Economic Review, 91*(5): 1423–1453.

the pure version of the model which assumes identical technologies across countries does not find much support in data, modified versions, which allow for some systematic technological differences across countries or significant endowment differences which would cause a breakdown of factor price equalization, find much stronger support in data. The model is more useful in thinking about the impact of international trade on factor prices. Furthermore, the result that international trade can produce winners and losers makes this an important model in the tool kit of economists.

Problem Set

Question 1

Consider an economy which is producing two goods computers (C) and shoes (S) using two factors of production capital and labor. To produce one computer, it requires 200 units of capital and 5 units of labor. To produce a pair of shoes, it requires 10 units of capital and 1 unit of labor. (Unlike the Cobb–Douglas production used in the text, here we are using fixed proportions (Leontief) production functions to make the math easier. That is, the 2 inputs are used in fixed proportions and cannot be substituted for each other)

(a) Calculate the capital/labor ratios used in computers and shoes. Which good is more capital-intensive?

Now, suppose the price of one computer is \$500 and the price of a pair of shoes is \$40.

(b) Using the information on goods prices and the production function for the two goods, calculate the wage and the rental rate of capital.
(c) Suppose the price of computer increases to \$650 but the price of shoes remains at \$40. Verify Stolper–Samuelson theorem.

Now, suppose the total amount of capital available in the economy is 8000 units and the total amount of labor available is 320 units.

(d) Calculate the amounts of capital and labor going into the computer production and the amounts of capital and labor going into the Shoes production.
(e) Based on the answer to part (d) calculate the amounts of computers and shoes produced in the economy.
(f) Now, suppose the total endowment of capital remains the same, but the total amount of labor increases to 500 units. What will happen to the amounts of computers and shoes produced compared to the results in part (e) above? Verify Rybczynski's theorem.

Question 2

Consider a country that produces two goods, wheat (W) and cotton (C), with two factors of production: land (T) and labor (L). The technology for wheat and cotton is as follows. Each unit of wheat requires 10 units of labor and 1 unit of land. Each unit of cotton requires 30 units of labor and 1 unit of land. Denote the wage by w and the rent of land by r.

a) Suppose a country has 500 units of labor and 20 units of land. Determine the allocation of labor and land between the two goods algebraically and then show it diagrammatically. How much wheat and cotton are produced in the economy?
b) Now, suppose that the labor supply increases to 540 units. Determine the allocation of labor and land between the two goods algebraically and then show them diagrammatically. Verify Rybczynski's theorem.
c) Now, suppose Malaysia has 500 units of labor and 20 units of land, while Indonesia has 80 units of land and 8000 units of labor. Which country has a comparative advantage in cotton? Which country has a comparative advantage in wheat? What is going to be the pattern of trade between these two countries?
d) Denote the price of cotton by P_C and the price of wheat by P_W. Suppose the autarky prices in the two countries are as follows. Malaysia: $P_C = 100$, $Pw = 40$. Indonesia: $P_C = 80$, $Pw = 60$. Calculate the autarky levels of wage and rent in both countries.

e) Now, suppose the world trading price of the two goods is $P_C = 90$, $Pw = 50$. Calculate the factor prices in both countries in a trading equilibrium. Verify the Stolper–Samuelson theorem.

Question 3

Look at the table below.

	Physical Capital	Researchers	Skilled Labor	Unskilled Labor	GDP
USA	25	26	27	2	20
China	10	17	8	18	15
apan	12	11	5.8	2	6
India	4	3	6	30	5
Germany	8	6	3	1	4.5

In the table above, each number represents a country's share in the world endowment of a factor production or GDP. For example, number 25 in the row for USA and the column for Physical Capital says that the US owns 25% of the world endowment of physical capital. Based on these numbers and your knowledge of the Heckscher–Ohlin model, answer the following questions:

a) Which countries should be exporting the services of Physical capital?
b) Which countries should be importing the services of Researchers?
c) Which countries should be exporting the services of skilled labor?
d) Which countries should be exporting the services of unskilled labor?

Question 4

There has been an increase in the wage inequality (gap between the skilled and unskilled wage) in the US and many European countries over the last 40 years. At the same time, these countries have increased their trade with China. Can international trade be a cause of the rising inequality? How can the Heckscher–Ohlin model help explain the rising inequality?

Question 5

According to the Heckscher-Ohlin model with 2 goods and 2 factors (capital and labor), the movement of Mexican migrants to the US would increase the production of the labor-intensive goods in the US. True or False? Explain your answer.

Chapter 4

Increasing Returns and Trade

4.1 Introduction

So far, we have looked at models of comparative advantage where international trade between countries was based on either productivity differences (Ricardian model) or endowment differences (Heckscher–Ohlin model). However, in the 1970s, empirical evidence documenting trade in very similar goods starts emerging. For example, the US both exported cars to Europe and imported cars from Europe. An extreme example is the two-way exchange of golf clubs between the US and its trading partners. This kind of trade became known as the "intra-industry" trade, which was difficult to explain based on the comparative advantage models. The most well-known model of intra-industry trade (IIT) is the Krugman model, which we describe in detail in this chapter.[1]

The Krugman model has two basic features as follows:

(1) Increasing returns to scale in production;
(2) Love of variety utility function.

Using these two features in a theoretical model, Paul Krugman, a Nobel Prize-winning economist, showed that countries can gain

[1]Our exposition of the Krugman model as well as the economics of Dumping follows the discussion of these topics in Krugman, P., Obstfeld, M., and Melitz, M. (2018). *International Economics* (11th edition), Pearson, chapter 8.

from trade even if they are exactly identical in all respects. Before going into the formal model, let us look at a simple numerical example to fix the ideas involved.

4.2 A Simple Numerical Example

Suppose the production function for cars exhibits increasing returns to scale as in Table 4.1. The increasing returns to scale in production means that if you double all inputs, the output more than doubles. Conversely, to double the output, the inputs need to be less than doubled. Now, suppose cars can be produced using a single input: labor. The amount of labor required to produce a given number of cars is given in Table 4.1. Assume that the unit of labor is the number of man-years (hours worked by a worker in a year, say 2000 h).

The numbers in Table 4.1 mean the following. To produce 50 cars, you need to use 100 units of labor, to produce 100 cars you need to use 150 units of labor and so on. Note that in going from 50 cars to 100 cars, the production of cars doubled but the amount of labor required less than doubled. Therefore, the production function exhibits increasing returns to scale. The third column captures the average labor input, which is simply the second column divided by the first column. The table also assumes that wage rate is $10,000 per man-year. Therefore, the average cost of producing a car is simply the average labor input multiplied by the wage rate. Thus, when 50 cars are produced, the average labor input is 2, and therefore, the average cost of producing a car is $20,000. Similarly, when 200 cars

Table 4.1: Production function and cost of producing cars.

Output	**Total labor input**	**Average labor input**	**Average cost**
50	100	2	20,000
100	150	1.5	15,000
150	200	1.33	13,330
200	250	1.25	12,500
250	300	1.2	12,000
300	350	1.166	11,660

are produced, the average labor input is 1.25 and hence the average cost of producing a car is $12,500.

Now, suppose there are two countries, Home and Foreign. In autarky (when they are not trading), each country produces and consumes 100 units of four different models of cars. Suppose Home produces models A, B, C and D and Foreign produces models J, K, L and M. Also assume that the price of a car in each country equals the average cost (this will be true if the market is monopolistically competitive, which we will assume in the formal model later). Since the average cost of cars when 100 units are produced is $15,000, the price of a car in each country is going to be $15,000 in autarky.

Now, let us assume that the two countries can trade with each other and exchange cars. That is, Home can export cars to Foreign and import cars from Foreign. Let us see what happens if each country continues to consume 100 units each of four models of cars. Suppose that now Home produces only A and B models but in larger quantities to meet both the Home demand and the export demand. Similarly, Foreign produces only J and K models but in larger quantities. To ensure that consumers in both countries have access to the four models in same quantities as in autarky, the production of each model should be 200. That is, suppose Home produces 200 units of A and B and Foreign produces 200 units of J and K. What will be the price of a car when 200 units of it are produced now? It is clear from Table 4.1 that the average cost of producing a car, when 200 units are produced, is $12,500. Therefore, consumers in both countries will continue to have access to four models (A, B, J and K) in 100 units each but at a lower price of $12,500 compared to the autarky price of $15,000. This is how the gains from trade arise in the Krugman model. Note that the gains from trade arise due to increasing returns in production. That is, the average cost of production decreases as firms produce at a larger scale, thereby moving down the average cost curve.

The simple example above overlooks several things which will be made clear in the formal model. For example, it is likely that consumers in both countries will have access to a larger number of varieties (more than four models) after opening up to trade than in autarky. If this is true, then the gains from trade will come not only from a lower price but also by having access to a larger number of varieties to choose from. One way to quickly see how more models can be produced is to note that after opening to trade, each country is using only 500 units of labor to produce the two models in larger quantities ($250 \times 2 = 500$). In autarky, each country was using 600 units of labor to produce cars. Recall that they were producing 100 units of four models each requiring $150 \times 4 = 600$ units of labor. After opening up to trade, they are using only 500 units of labor. So, the 100 units of labor that is freed up can be used to produce more cars.

4.3 The Formal Model

Having discussed the intuition behind the Krugman model through an earlier numerical example, we now discuss a formal model. As mentioned before, one key feature of the Krugman model is increasing returns to scale in production. Rather than positing a production function exhibiting increasing returns to scale, we directly work with a cost function based on an increasing returns to scale production function. Assume the total cost function to take the following form:

$$TC(Q) = F + C * Q.$$

In the above equation, TC denotes total cost, F denotes fixed cost, C denotes marginal cost and Q denotes the output of the firm. Note from the above total cost function that the marginal cost, MC, is constant at C. The average cost function is given as

$$AC(Q) = F/Q + C.$$

Therefore, as the firm output increases, the average cost of production decreases as shown in Figure 4.1.

Since $MC < AC$, if the market is perfectly competitive, $P = MC < AC$, and hence, firms would make losses. That is, perfect competition is incompatible with increasing returns to scale in production. Therefore, we will assume an imperfectly competitive market structure. In particular, we assume a monopolistically competitive market that has elements of both monopoly and competition. The monopolistic element of the market arises from the fact that each firm faces a downward-sloping demand curve, which gives it some

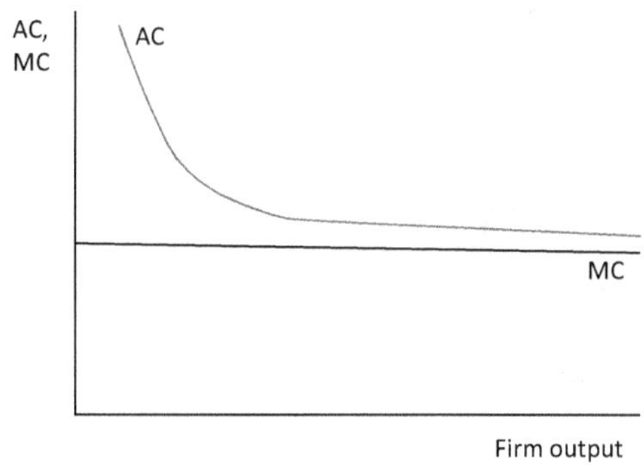

Figure 4.1: Average and marginal cost.

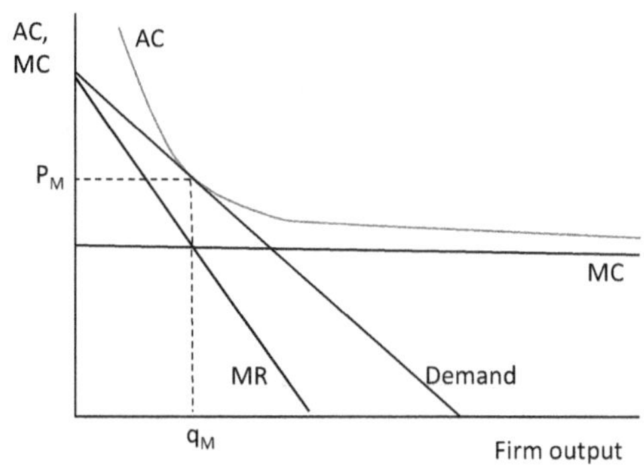

Figure 4.2: Equilibrium with monopolistic competition.

market power in setting prices. The competitive element comes from the assumption of free entry and exit, which leads to zero profits in equilibrium. Therefore, the equilibrium in the market is going to be characterized by the following two conditions:

(1) $MR = MC$ (Marginal Revenue = Marginal Cost) (Profit Maximization Condition);
(2) $P = AC$ (Price = Average Cost) (Zero-Profit Condition).

Figure 4.2 shows the textbook representation of equilibrium in a monopolistically competitive market.

To specify the equilibrium in our model, we need to specify the demand curve that the firms are facing.

4.3.1 *Demand side*

We assume that each firm i faces the following demand function:

$$Q_i = S\left[\frac{1}{n} - b(P_i - \bar{P})\right],$$

where Q_i is the demand for variety – i, S is the total sales (market demand for the good), n is the number of firms (varieties), P_i is the price charged by firm i, $\bar{P}$ is the average price charged by the other firms, b is the slope parameter.[2]

Note from the above demand function that if $P_i = \bar{P}$, then the firm sells amount S/n. If the firm charges a lower price, $P_i < \bar{P}$, it sells more than S/n. On the contrary, if it charges $P_i > \bar{P}$, then it sells less than S/n. How much more or less depends on the slope parameter b which captures the sensitivity of firm demand to firm price: $\frac{dQ_i}{dP_i} = -bS$.

Having described the key elements of the model, we discuss the autarky equilibrium next.

4.3.2 *Autarky equilibrium n and P*

As mentioned earlier, the equilibrium is characterized by the two conditions: $MR = MC$ and $P = AC$.

In what follows, we derive the expression for MR from the demand curve for the firm specified earlier, which we recall is

$$Q_i = S\left[\frac{1}{n} - b(P_i - \bar{P})\right].$$

Denoting total revenue by TR, we write $MR = \frac{d(TR)}{dQ_i}$, where $TR = P * Q$. Therefore,

$$MR = P + Q\left(\frac{dP}{dQ}\right) = P\left(1 + \frac{Q}{P}\frac{dP}{dQ}\right).$$

---

[2]See Krugman, P., Obstfeld, M., and Melitz, M. (2018). *International Economics* (11th edition), Pearson, 175–176, for a deeper discussion of this demand curve.

Now from the demand function, note that $\frac{dQ_i}{dP_i} = -bS$. Therefore,

$$MR = P\left[1 + \frac{Q}{P}\left(-\frac{1}{bS}\right)\right] = P - \frac{Q}{bS},$$

where we are suppressing the subscript i because all firms are identical. Given the above expression for MR, our profit maximization condition becomes

$$MR = MC \Rightarrow P - \frac{Q}{bS} = C. \tag{4.1}$$

In the above expression, the mathematical symbol "$\Rightarrow$" means "implies". Next, symmetry implies that in any equilibrium all firms will sell the same quantity: Symmetry $\Rightarrow S/Q = n$. Therefore,

$$MR = MC \Rightarrow P - \frac{1}{nb} = C \Rightarrow P = C + \frac{1}{nb} \quad (MR = MC \text{ condition}).$$

Intuitively, higher $n \Rightarrow$ more competition $\Rightarrow$ lower markup (higher elasticity of demand) $\Rightarrow$ lower price.

Similarly, our zero-profit condition is given by

$$P = AC = \frac{F}{Q} + C. \tag{4.2}$$

Again, using $S/Q = n$, the above equation can be written as

$$P = \frac{nF}{S} + C \quad (P = AC \text{ condition}).$$

Intuitively, higher $n \Rightarrow$ lower S/n or lower output per firm which implies higher AC and, consequently, higher P.

We can diagrammatically determine the equilibrium n and P using Equations (4.1) and (4.2) in the (n, P) space. We can also easily verify that the $MR = MC$ condition gives a downward-sloping relationship in the (n, P) space denoted by MMC in Figure 4.3. The $P = AC$ condition gives an upward-sloping relationship in the (n, P) space denoted by PAC in Figure 4.3. Therefore, the intersection of the two determines the equilibrium values of n and P denoted by n^* and P^* in Figure 4.3.

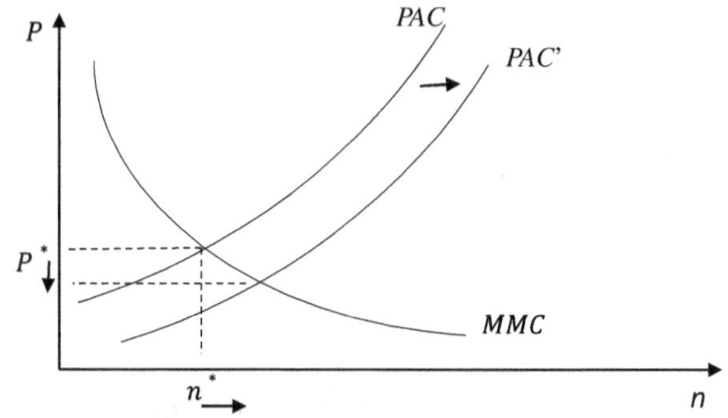

Figure 4.3: Autarky equilibrium.

4.3.2.1 *Comparative statics*

Next, we study how the equilibrium values of n and P change as the market size, S, increases. This exercise is known as comparative statics. We can do this diagrammatically. When S increases, there is no change in the $MR = MC$ condition; thus, the line MMC remains unchanged. However, the $P = AC$ condition does change. We can easily verify from the $P = AC$ condition that an increase in S implies a lower P for each n. Therefore, the PAC curve shifts down or to the right. As a result, the equilibrium value of n increases and the equilibrium value of P decreases as shown in Figure 4.3.

The above result can be shown algebraically as follows:

Use the two equations $(MR = MC)$ $P = C + \frac{1}{nb}$ and $(P = AC)$ $P = \frac{nF}{S} + C$ to obtain $C + \frac{1}{nb} = \frac{nF}{S} + C$, and hence $n^2 = \frac{S}{bF}$, which implies $n = \sqrt{\frac{S}{bF}}$. Therefore, $\frac{dn}{n} = \frac{1}{2}\frac{dS}{S} > 0$ {a 10% increase in S leads to a 5% increase in n}. The expression for P is given by $P = \sqrt{\frac{F}{bS}} + C$, and therefore, $\frac{dP}{P} = -\frac{1}{2}\frac{dS}{S} < 0$.

More generally, denoting the equilibrium values of n and P by n^* and P^*, we have shown that

$$\frac{dn^*}{dS} > 0; \quad \frac{dP^*}{dS} < 0.$$

That is, an increase in the market size increases the equilibrium number of firms and decreases the equilibrium price. Therefore, consumers in a larger market gain from having access to a larger number of varieties at a lower price.

In Section 4.3.3, we discuss the impact of trade in this model.

4.3.3 *Increasing returns and trade*

Let us now bring in two countries: Home and Foreign. Use subscripts H and F to denote the variables for Home and Foreign, respectively. Firms in both countries face identical technologies and consumers have identical preferences. The market sizes in the two countries are S_{H} and S_{F}, which can be equal or different. Denote the autarky number of firms (varieties) and the average price in the two countries by $(n_{\mathrm{H}}, P_{\mathrm{H}})$ and $(n_{\mathrm{F}}, P_{\mathrm{F}})$, respectively.

When the two countries integrate, the size of the market becomes $S_{\mathrm{H}} + S_{\mathrm{F}}$, which we denote by S_{I}, where the subscript I denotes the "integrated" economy. Since $S_{\mathrm{I}} > S_{\mathrm{H}}$ and $S_{\mathrm{I}} > S_{\mathrm{F}}$, it follows from the results derived earlier that $n_{\mathrm{I}} > n_{\mathrm{H}}$, $n_{\mathrm{I}} > n_{\mathrm{F}}$ and $P_{\mathrm{I}} < P_{\mathrm{H}}$, $P_{\mathrm{I}} < P_{\mathrm{F}}$.

Thus, we have proved that the number of firms (varieties) in the integrated economy is larger than in either country in autarky and the average price in the integrated economy is lower than that in either country in autarky. Therefore, consumers in both countries gain from having access to a larger number of varieties at a lower price. This is the key idea of the Krugman model.

In Section 4.4, we provide some empirical evidence on gains from trade based on increasing returns to scale.

4.4 Empirical Evidence on Gains from Trade with IRS

Canadian economy is much smaller than the US economy, and hence, its automobile firms were much smaller than those in the US when they were mainly producing for the domestic market. In 1964, the US and Canada agreed to have free trade in automobiles and automobile parts. Economists have studied the impact of this on the automobile sector in the two countries.[3] Before the pact, the

[3]This discussion is based on the case study in Krugman, P., Obstfeld, M., and Melitz, M. (2018). *International Economics* (11th edition), Pearson, 186–187.

productivity in Canada (output per worker) was 30% less than that in the US. Canada exported automobile products worth \$16 million and imported automobile products worth \$519 million in 1962. By 1968, Canadian export increased to \$2.4 billion and imports increased to \$2.9 billion. By the early 1970s, Canadian productivity had almost equalled the US productivity. The reason was that Canadian automakers were producing for the much larger US–Canada market and as a result producing at a much larger scale, which allowed them to move down their average cost curves.

The US–Canada automobile pact eventually led to the US–Canada free trade agreement in 1988 and Mexico joined it in 1994 to make it the North American Free Trade Agreement (NAFTA). As a consequence of NAFTA, the manufacture of automobile parts was consolidated throughout the North American market. There is evidence that in the first decade following NAFTA, trade in automotive parts between the United States and Mexico more than doubled in both directions and then doubled again in the following decade. This highlights the importance of intra-industry trade (IIT) in the automobile industry.

4.5 Intra-Industry Trade

As mentioned earlier, the model developed above is suitable for studying trade within industries such as the automobile industry, the electronics industry, etc. One way to measure the importance of IIT is to construct an index called the "Index of IIT".

IIT can be measured in two alternative ways, both giving the same result.

$$\text{IIT} = 1 - \frac{|X - M|}{X + M} = 1 - \frac{\text{gap}}{\text{volume}},$$

where X is exports, M is imports, $X - M$ is the trade gap and $X + M$ is the total trade volume.

Alternatively, we can write IIT as

$$\text{IIT} = 2\,\frac{\text{Min}\{X, M\}}{X + M}.$$

It is easy to verify that the range of IIT is from 0 to 1, where 0 indicates no IIT and 1 indicates full IIT. IIT of 0 implies that the country either exports the good or imports the good but not both. IIT of 1, on the contrary, implies that the country's exports and imports in that industry are balanced (exports = imports).

4.5.1 *Intra- and inter-industry trade*

To understand intra- and inter-industry trade more clearly, let us think of two industries — agriculture and manufacturing. Suppose there are two factors of production, capital and land. Manufacturing is capital intensive while agriculture is land intensive. Also assume that Home is capital abundant and Foreign is land abundant. From our knowledge of the Heckscher–Ohlin model we know that Home has a comparative advantage in manufacturing and Foreign has a comparative advantage in agriculture. Now, if there is no IIT, then Home exports manufacturing and Foreign exports agriculture. Assuming a balanced trade, Figure 4.4 shows that the trade flow in each direction is worth \$100 million. This is how inter-industry trade looks like.

Now suppose manufacturing production exhibits increasing returns to scale and consumers have a love for variety as discussed earlier. Now, there will be two-way trade in manufacturing. As a result, the trade between the two countries can look something like

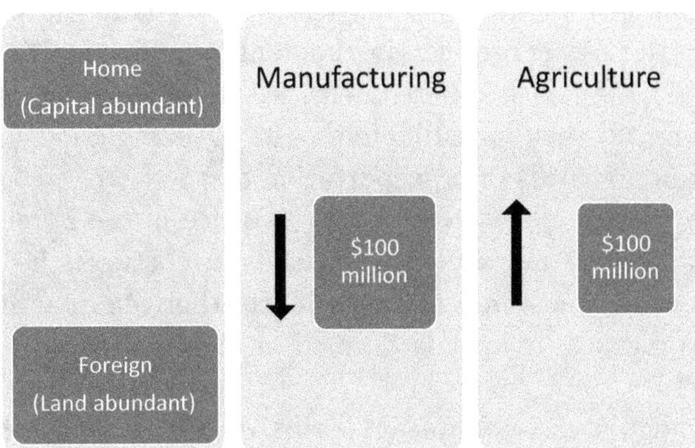

Figure 4.4: Inter-industry trade only.

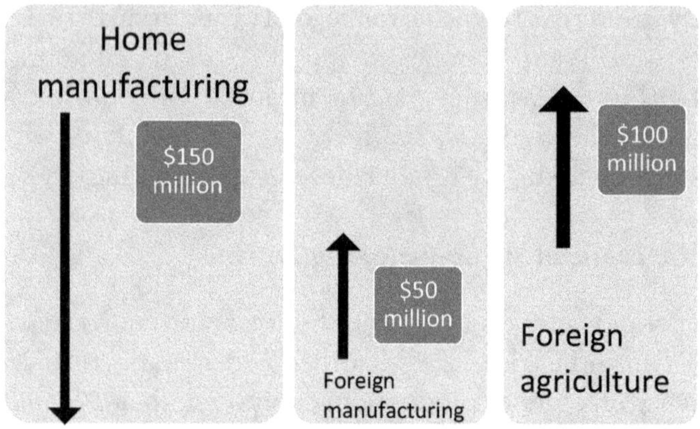

Figure 4.5: Inter- and intra-industry trade.

that shown in Figure 4.5 where now Home exports manufacturing worth \$150 million to Foreign and Foreign exports agriculture worth \$100 million. But now Foreign also exports manufacturing worth \$50 million. We can calculate the index of IIT from these numbers. The index of IIT in manufacturing is 0.5.

Having discussed the Krugman model and the IIT, we next turn to an application of the imperfect competition model to international trade called dumping.

4.6 Dumping

When firms sell in different markets, they could charge different prices for the same product in different markets for two possible reasons: (1) they face different elasticities of demand in different markets and (2) they have different costs of selling goods in different markets due to tariffs or transportation cost.

When a firm sells a good at a lower price in the Foreign market than in its Home market or when the gap between its price and marginal cost (mark-up) is lower in the Foreign market than in the Home market, then it is deemed as dumping by anti-dumping authorities.

Dumping is an example of price discrimination where firms charge different prices in different markets because of either differing price elasticities of demand or the different cost of serving the two markets.

Suppose a firm sells in the Home market as well as in the Foreign market. There is no additional cost of serving the Foreign market. In this case, the profit maximization condition for the firm is $MR_{\mathrm{H}} = MR_{\mathrm{F}} = MC$, where the subscript i = H, F refers to Home and Foreign, respectively. The condition above says that the marginal revenue must be equalized in each market, which must in turn equal the marginal cost. This is a generalization of the standard profit maximization condition, $MR = MC$, to the case when a firm sells in multiple markets. Intuitively, if the marginal revenue is higher in one market than the other, then the firm should sell more in the market with a higher marginal revenue. Profit is maximized only when there is no scope of shifting sales from one market to another, which happens only when the marginal revenues in the two markets are equalized.

Let us diagrammatically look at the equilibrium of a firm selling in two different markets. To show the case of dumping where a firm sells at a lower price in the Foreign market than in the Home market, we assume that the elasticity of demand in the Foreign market is higher than that in the Home market. One easy way to capture this diagrammatically is to use a horizontal demand curve for the Foreign market and a downward-sloping demand curve for the Home market, labeled D_{F} and D_{H}, respectively in Figure 4.6.

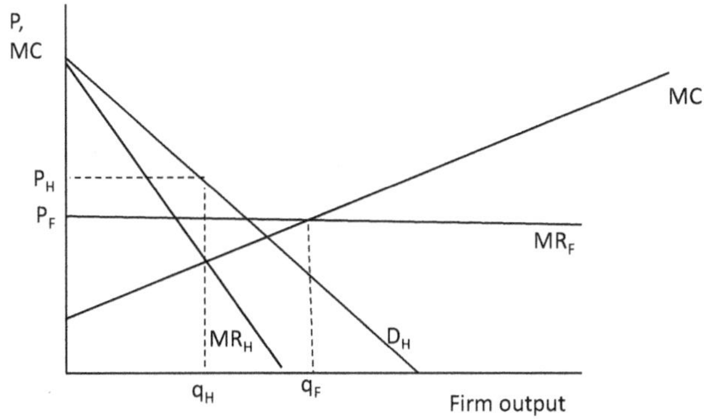

Figure 4.6: Dumping.

Since the horizontal demand curve has an elasticity of ∞, the elasticity of D_F is higher than any point on the demand curve, D_H. The marginal revenue curve corresponding to D_F is the same as D_F, while the marginal revenue curve corresponding to D_H is MR_H. We assume an upward-sloping MC curve. That is, the marginal cost of the firm is increasing in output.

Now the profit-maximizing condition $MR_H = MR_F = MC$ is satisfied for the firm when it sells q_H in the Home market and q_F in the Foreign market (where the amount q_F is the distance from the point q_H to q_F in Figure 4.6) and charges a price of P_H in the Home market and P_F in the Foreign market. Clearly, $P_H > P_F$, which may be deemed as dumping. The reason for dumping (or $P_H > P_F$) is that the firm faces a more elastic demand in the Foreign market.

4.6.1 *Alternative model of dumping*

Next, we look at an alternative case of dumping where the demand curves facing the firm in the Home and Foreign markets are identical, but the costs are different. Assume that the firm has a constant marginal cost of $MC_H = C$ for serving the Home market. However, there is an additional trading cost of t, per unit, for serving the Foreign market. The trading cost can arise due to transportation cost as well as trade barriers. So, the effective marginal cost for serving the Foreign market becomes $MC_F = C + t$. Figure 4.7 shows the profit-maximizing prices in the two markets. Clearly, $MC_F > MC_H$ implies $P_F > P_H$.

Now define $P_H - C$ as the markup of the firm in the Home market and $P_F - (C + t)$ as the markup in the Foreign market. It can be verified that the markup varies inversely with the elasticity of demand. For example, in a competitive market, $\varepsilon = \infty$ and $P = MC$ or markup = zero. Recall that along a linear demand the elasticity of demand keeps decreasing as we move down the demand curve. This implies that the markup is lower in the Foreign market than in the Home market

$$P_F - (C + t) < P_H - C \quad \text{or} \quad P_F - t < P_H.$$

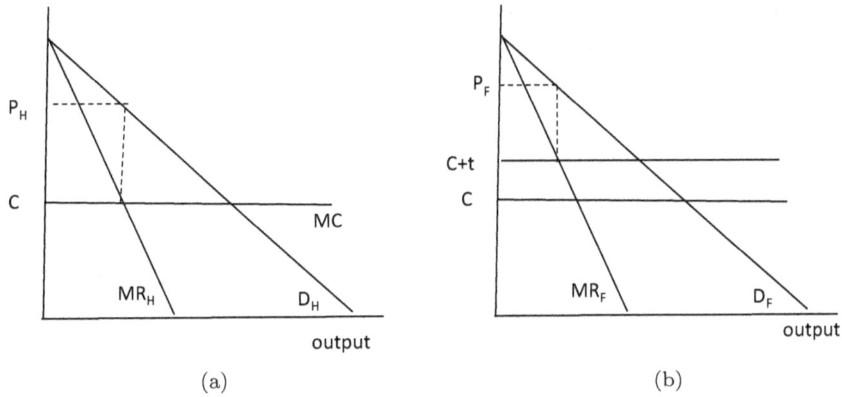

Figure 4.7: Alternative model of dumping.

That is, the price charged by the firm net of trading cost is lower in the Foreign market than in the Home market. This will qualify as dumping under current rules because the net price that the firm actually receives from selling in the Foreign market is less than the net price it receives in the Home market.

The above analysis shows that there is nothing sinister about dumping. It may simply be the profit-maximizing strategy of a firm selling in different markets facing different elasticities of demand. However, this is not to deny the possibility of a foreign firm engaging in predatory pricing to drive competitors out of a market with the aim of raising the price once the competitors are out.

Visit the USITC website at https://www.usitc.gov to see the anti-dumping cases undergoing investigation in the United States. For example, in the recent years, China has been subject to anti-dumping duties on: TVs, furniture, crepe paper, hand trucks, shrimp, ironing tables, plastic shopping bags, iron pipe fittings, saccharin, solar panels, tires and cold-rolled steel.

4.7 Concluding Remarks

For a long time, economists believed that international trade among countries was driven by comparative advantage. However, the Krugman model changed this thinking showing that countries could trade and gain from trade even if they are identical provided production functions exhibit increasing returns to scale and consumers have a taste for variety. This model had an enormous impact on the field of international trade. More recently, Marc Melitz, in an influential paper published in *Econometrica* in 2003,[4] introduced firm heterogeneity in the Krugman model. In the original Krugman model, all firms are identical. However, in reality, firms differ in their productivities. Melitz showed that if firms have heterogeneous productivities, then international trade can provide additional gains. In particular, international trade between countries leads to the exit of many low-productivity firms from each country and the resources freed up by these firms are used by higher productivity firms, which improves the overall productivity of the economy. A lot of empirical work has found support for this theoretical model.

Problem Set

Question 1

Suppose that the demand facing firms producing Golf clubs in Home and Foreign is given as follows:

$$Q_i = S\left[\frac{1}{n} - b(P_i - \bar{P})\right]$$

The cost of producing Golf clubs is given by

$$TC(Q_i) = F + C * Q_i$$

a) Assume that the parameters for Home are as follows: $S_H = 1440$, $b = 2$, $F = 5$, $C = 1$. Compute the equilibrium values of n, P, and Q. {Hint: either derive the expression for marginal revenue from the demand curve above or use the expression for marginal revenue from the text.}

[4] Melitz, M. J. (2003). The impact of trade on intra-industry reallocations and aggregate industry productivity, *Econometrica*, *71*(6).

b) Assume that the parameters for Foreign are as follows: $S_F = 250$, $b = 2$, $F = 5$, $C = 1$. Compute the equilibrium values of n, P, and Q for Foreign.

c) Now, suppose that Home and Foreign trade freely in Golf clubs. What are the equilibrium values of n, P, and Q in the integrated economy? Is trade welfare improving for consumers in both countries? Justify your answer.

Question 2

Suppose that a Chinese solar panel manufacturer has an upward sloping marginal cost function given by $MC = 10Q$, where Q is the total number of solar panels produced by this firm. Denote the number of panels sold in the Chinese market by Q_H and the number of panels sold in the US market by Q_F. The firm faces a downward sloping demand curve in the Chinese market given by $P_H = 750 - 5Q_H$. It faces a horizontal demand curve in the US market at a price of 500. That is, it can sell any number of panels in the US market at that price.

a) How many panels will the firm sell in each market?

b) What is the profit-maximizing price of the panels it charges in the Chinese market?

c) Is the price in the Chinese market higher or lower than in the US market? Will this qualify as dumping?

d) Show the results diagrammatically.

Question 3

Here is a list of products: rice, wheat, gold, automobiles, golf clubs, wine, and movies. For each of these products, explain whether you expect the trade to be inter-industry trade or intra-industry trade.

Chapter 5

Movement of Factors of Production

5.1 Introduction

In the first four chapters, we studied international trade but assumed that the factors of production such as labor and capital do not move across international borders. In this chapter, we study the implications of movements of two factors of production, labor and capital, between countries. In particular, we study what determines the movements of these factors of production and what are the welfare implications of these movements. We first look at the movement of labor and then the movement of capital.

5.2 Movement of Labor

The movement of labor between countries is called migration. According to the UN report on immigration (2015), about 3.3% of the world population lives in a country different from their country of birth. Among rich countries, the percentage of population that is foreign born is 43% in Singapore, 33% in Australia, 22% in Canada and about 14% in the US. While people move across countries all the time for various reasons, there are some episodes of large migration in history which allow economists to study the economic implications of migration. Here are a couple of examples of large waves of migration which have been studied by economists. In September 1980, about 125,000 Cubans migrated from Cuba to the city of Miami, which led

Table 5.1: Numerical example on migration.

# of workers	Total output	Marginal output	Average output
1	100	100	100
2	190	90	95
3	270	80	90
4	340	70	85
5	400	60	80
6	450	50	75
7	490	40	70
8	520	30	65
9	540	20	60
10	550	10	55

to a 7% increase in the population of Miami and a 20% increase in the Cuban population of Miami. This episode of migration is known as the "Mariel Boat lift". Following the breakup of the Soviet Union, between 1989 and 1996, about 670,000 Russian Jews moved to Israel. This increased the population of Israel by 11% and its workforce by 14%. These are very large shocks to the labor force of a city or a country, making them suitable for studying the implications of migration.

Now, we study the implications of migration using a simple numerical example and a picture. Suppose that each country produces a single good, food, using land and labor. The production function for food is given in Table 5.1, which shows how the amount of food produced varies as the number of workers increases, keeping the amount of land fixed. As can be clearly seen from column 3 in Table 5.1, the production function exhibits diminishing marginal product of labor. That is, as an increasing amount of labor is added to a fixed amount of land, the extra output produced by the additional unit of labor declines.

Now, suppose that there are 2 countries: Home and Foreign. To keep things simple, assume that each country has the same amount of land (what is needed for the result is that the land–labor ratio should be different across countries). However, Home has only three

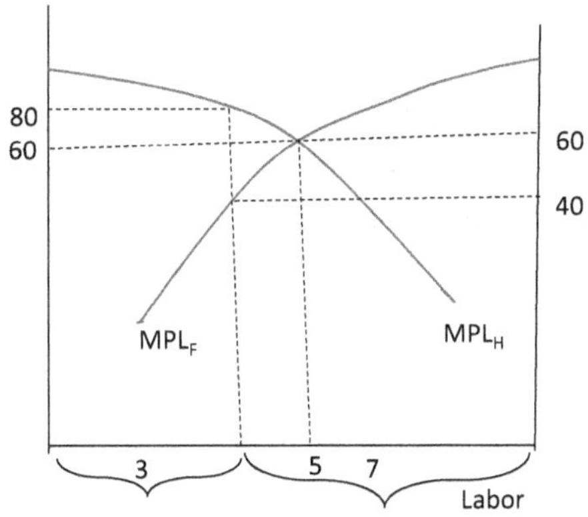

Figure 5.1: Impact of immigration.

units of labor, while Foreign has seven units of labor. Assume that the labor market is perfectly competitive in both countries. As a result, the wage of labor equals the marginal product of labor.

Since Home has three units of labor and the marginal product of the third unit of labor is 80, the wage in Home is 80 units of food. Note that the output in Home is 270 units of food. Since there are three workers each getting a wage of 80, the total wage bill is 240. Therefore, the reward of land is 270 – 240 = 30, which goes to the landowners. That is, out of a total output of 270, the amount going to workers is 240 and the amount going to landowners is 30. In Figure 5.1, the curve labeled MPL_H is the marginal product of labor in Home where labor in Home is measured from the left axis and labor in Foreign is measured from the right axis. The area under the MPL_H curve to the left of $L = 3$ is the total output of 270. The rectangle formed by wage $= 80$ and $L = 3$ is the total wage bill and the area below the MPL_H curve and above this rectangle is the reward of the landowners.

Similarly, since Foreign has seven units of labor, the total output is 490, while the marginal output for the seventh unit of labor is 40. As a result, the wage is 40 as well. Therefore, the total wage bill is 280 and the reward of the landowners in Foreign is $490 - 280 = 210$ and the corresponding areas are shown in Figure 5.1. This is the situation before migration.

What happens if workers are allowed to move across international borders? Since the wage in Home is greater than the wage in Foreign, workers in Foreign would like to migrate to Home. This is a model of economic migration where the sole driver of migration is the wage differential between the two countries. Given this, workers from Foreign will continue to move to Home as long as there is a wage differential. The post-migration equilibrium is restored when the wages are equalized across countries. This happens when two workers move from Foreign to Home.

5.2.1 *Impact of migration on Home and Foreign*

What is the impact of inward migration on workers and landowners in Home? As the number of workers increases from 3 to 5, the wage in Home decreases from 80 to 60. The total output increases to 400, and the wage bill increases to 300. The difference of the two is the reward of the landowners. Therefore, the reward of the landowners increases from 30 to 100. As a consequence, landowners gain from migration, whereas native workers lose in Home. The migrant workers gain in Home because they earned a wage of 40 in Foreign before migration but now earn 60 in Home. In Foreign, the wage increases from 40 to 60; therefore, the workers who stay behind in Foreign gain. The reward of the landowners in Foreign decreases from 210 to 100 because the total output in Foreign decreases to 400, while the wage bill increases to 300. What happens to the world output? It is clear from the numbers in the table that the world output increases from 760 to 800; therefore, there are overall gains from migration.

This simple model captures the essence of the economics of migration. The results suggest that migration produces winners and losers, but there are overall gains from it. Native workers in Home, who have to compete with migrants, lose but landowners gain. The opposite happens in Foreign. Since migration produces winners and losers, one can expect political opposition to migration which can be exploited by populist politicians. During the Brexit referendum in Britain and the Presidential election in the US in 2016, immigration was a key issue and the anti-immigrant sentiments of voters may have affected the voting outcomes.

5.2.2 *Empirical evidence on the impact of migration*

Economic historian Jeffrey Williamson has studied the impact of migration between Europe and the new world countries between 1870 and 1913 on the wages of workers in both the source countries (European countries) and the destination (United States, Argentina, Canada and Australia).[1] He found that the real wage growth was much faster in the source countries than the host countries. For example, the real wage increased by 47% in the US over this period, but it increased by 250% in Sweden. Is this consistent with the theoretical model we studied earlier? Recall that our model suggested that the real wage increases in the source country but decreases in the destination countries. This prediction would hold true in a world where there is no productivity growth. When productivity growth is taking place, as was the case during 1870–1913, we would expect real wage to increase everywhere. However, we would expect migration to slow down real wage growth in destination countries and accelerate it in source countries, which is exactly what Williamson found with the exception of Canada, which despite being a destination country experienced a 121% increase in real wage which was larger than what was experienced by source countries such as Ireland and Italy. But the evidence was broadly consistent with the simple theoretical model presented here.

There is also evidence of convergence in the real wages of workers between the Western European countries and the new member states in Eastern Europe following the enlargement of the European union over the period 1997–2015.

Looking at the recent impact of immigration on wages in the US, economists Gianmarco Ottaviano and Giovanni Peri made the following findings in a paper published in the *Journal of European Economic Association* in 2012.[2] The large-scale immigration of low-skilled workers has put a downward pressure on the wages

[1]Williamson, J. (1995). The evolution of global labor markets since 1830: Background evidence and hypotheses. *Explorations in Economic History, 32*(2): 141–196.

[2]Ottaviano, G. I. P. and Peri, G. (2012). Rethinking the effect of immigration on wages. *Journal of the European Economic Association, 10*: 152–197.

of less educated native workers, but the effects are quantitatively small. However, the wages of more educated workers have increased, with the overall effect of immigration on wages being positive. The findings suggest that the low-skilled immigrants are substitutes for less educated native workers and complements for more educated native workers. In terms of our model, we can replace landowners by high-skilled or more educated workers and think of the two factors of production as low-skilled and high-skilled workers. In this setting, immigration of low-skilled workers would put a downward pressure on the wages of native low-skilled workers and benefit native high-skilled workers (just as landowners benefited in our theoretical model).

Immigration can also provide gains through channels not discussed in our theoretical model. For example, in many countries, such as the Philippines, Mexico and Guatemala, immigrants send large amounts of money (remittances) home, which allows their families that stay back to invest in education, start a business or build a home. Sometimes, immigration can increase human capital accumulation by people in the source country because it improves their chances of migrating abroad. This has been observed clearly in the case of Fiji where large-scale migration by Indian origin people to Australia and New Zealand following ethnic troubles in the late 1980s increased the schooling of the people left behind.

Finally, migration could enrich the culture of the destination country as immigrants bring with them their customs, food, dress, etc. There is a folklore that when the Parsis (Zoroastrians) arrived on the western coast of India from Iran around 10th century, their leader went to the local ruler to ask for shelter. The local ruler showed him a cup of milk full to the brim and said that his land is already full like the cup. Then, the leader of the Parsis took a spoon of sugar and put it in the milk and stirred it. He told the ruler that just as the sugar dissolved in the milk and made it sweet, his people will also dissolve in the community and sweeten it without anyone noticing. The ruler allowed them to stay.

Having looked at the movement of labor, we turn our attention to the movement of capital.

5.3 Movement of Capital

We first learn about international borrowing and lending and then learn about Foreign Direct Investment (FDI). International borrowing and lending refers to situations where the borrower and the lender belong to different countries. One way to gauge the importance of international borrowing and lending or international capital flows is to look at the international investment position (IIP) of a country. This refers to the difference between a country's external financial assets and liabilities. When the IIP is positive, a country is a net lender, while a negative IIP suggests that a country is a net borrower. The IMF provides data on the IIP–GDP ratio for different countries. According to the recent IMF data, the ratio was 15.6 for China and –46.5 for the US. That is, China's net external financial assets are 15.6% of its GDP, while America's net financial liabilities are 46.5% of its GDP.

5.3.1 *International borrowing and lending*

Since borrowing and lending by necessity has an intertemporal dimension, whereby you borrow from someone today with a promise to pay back with interest in the future, we discuss its determinants using a model of two goods: present consumption and future consumption.

Before going into the details of the two-good model, let us look at some accounting identities which will help establish a link between trade balance of a country and international borrowing and lending. The basic national accounting identity for an open economy is given by

$$Y = C + I + G + NX,$$

where Y is the income, C is the consumption, I is the investment, G is the government expenditure and NX is the net exports (exports–imports). This identity simply says that the income equals expenditure. To keep things simple, assume that the government consumption is counted in C and government investment is counted in I, then the above is given by

$$Y = C + I + NX.$$

Next, rearrange the above to obtain

$$S \equiv Y - C = I + NX,$$

where S is saving, which equals the difference between income and consumption. Next, rewrite the above as

$$S - I = NX.$$

The above equality says that the trade balance of a country reflects its saving–investment gap. That is, if a country's savings exceed investments, then it runs a trade surplus: $NX > 0$. Alternatively, if investments exceed savings, then the country runs a trade deficit: $NX < 0$. If a country's savings exceed investments, the country lends its extra savings abroad, which is reflected in a trade surplus. That is, international lending and trade surplus are two sides of the same coin. Similarly, if savings fall short of the investment, the gap must be met by international borrowing, which is reflected in a trade deficit.

Given the discussion above, to understand why a country is a lender or a borrower in the international capital market, we have to understand why savings exceed investments or vice versa. To understand this, we bring in the two-good model mentioned earlier. Suppose that countries produce two goods: present consumption and future consumption.[3] They have some resources (land, labor, capital, etc.) which they can use to produce these two goods. The present consumption goods are those which are for current consumption such as food and clothing. The future consumption goods can be thought of as investment goods which will increase the productivity of the economy in the future such as roads, ports, railway, education and research.

---

[3]This model originally appears in Irving Fisher (1930). The theory of interest. New York: Macmillan. Our discussion is similar to that in Krugman, P., Obstfeld, M., and Melitz, M. (2018). *International Economics* (11th edition), Pearson, chapter 6.

Just as we can draw the production possibility frontier (PPF) of a country between say agriculture and manufacturing, we can also draw a PPF between present consumption and future consumption. What is the slope of the PPF? Since we plot present consumption on the horizontal axis and future consumption on the vertical axis, the slope of the PPF is the change in future consumption over the change in present consumption, or how much future consumption one has to give up to get one more unit of present consumption. This is the rate of transformation between present consumption and future consumption. This depends on the returns on investment in a country. If a country has great investment opportunities, then diverting resources from present consumption to future consumption is very attractive. That is, the return on investment is very high. Let us denote the net return on investment by r. That is, if resources are diverted from one unit of present consumption, they yield $1 + r$ units of future consumption. Note that as we move down the PPF, its slope increases in absolute value. That is, the return on investment becomes higher as we move down the PPF, or the opportunity cost of present consumption in terms of future consumption foregone increases as we move down the PPF. Alternatively, as we move up the PPF, the return on investment decreases because resources will be diverted to higher yielding projects first.

Denote by P_{C} the price of present consumption and by P_{F} the price of future consumption. Define $\frac{P_{\mathrm{C}}}{P_{\mathrm{F}}}$ as the relative price of present consumption. Given the PPF and the prices of the two goods, the economy would want to maximize the value of output: Value $= P_{\mathrm{C}}Q_{\mathrm{C}} + P_{\mathrm{F}}Q_{\mathrm{F}}$, where Q_{C} and Q_{F} are the respective quantities of the two goods produced. The value of output in terms of the future consumption, denoted by V, is given by $V = \frac{P_{\mathrm{C}}}{P_{\mathrm{F}}}Q_{\mathrm{C}} + Q_{\mathrm{F}}$. For a given relative price $\frac{P_{\mathrm{C}}}{P_{\mathrm{F}}}$, the value of output is maximized at the point of tangency between the PPF and an isovalue line with a slope $\frac{P_{\mathrm{C}}}{P_{\mathrm{F}}}$. Since the slope of the PPF is $1 + r$ as discussed earlier, at the point of tangency, it is the case that $\frac{P_{\mathrm{C}}}{P_{\mathrm{F}}} = 1 + r$.

So far, we have discussed how the value-maximizing point on the PPF can be found for a given relative price $\frac{P_{\mathrm{C}}}{P_{\mathrm{F}}}$. How is the price

$\frac{P_C}{P_F}$ determined? To do so, we bring in the preferences of consumers between present consumption and future consumption. This can be simply thought of as the decision of a consumer to allocate his/her income between consumption and saving. Whatever is saved will earn a rate of interest, which will finance future consumption. If a consumer is very impatient, he/she will consume most of the income today and save very little. Alternatively, a patient consumer will save a lot and consume less today. A higher rate of interest will make saving more attractive relative to present consumption. Therefore, from a consumer's point of view, the rate of interest on savings is the relative price of present consumption. Thus, suppose that the rate of interest is r, then the consumer effectively faces a relative price of present consumption of $1 + r$. That is, by consuming one unit of present consumption, the consumer is sacrificing $1 + r$ units of future consumption. Therefore, from the consumer's point of view, $\frac{P_C}{P_F} = 1+r$, where r is the rate of interest on saving. A consumer with an income I in terms of future consumption will face the following budget constraint: $I = \frac{P_C}{P_F}C_C + C_F$, where C_C and C_F denote the quantities of present and future consumption, respectively. Given the budget constraint, the consumer maximizes utility where the budget constraint is tangent to the highest possible indifference curve.

For the economy as a whole, the total value of output, V, must equal the income of the representative consumer, I. Therefore, for the economy as a whole, we can determine the optimal point on the PPF by simply superimposing the indifference map of the representative consumer and finding the point of tangency between the indifference curve and the PPF. The common slope of the indifference curve and the PPF is the equilibrium relative price $\frac{P_C}{P_F}$, which equals the rate of return on investment, which in turn equals the rate of return on saving from the point of view of consumers. The equilibrium is depicted in Figure 5.2.

Now, let us think of two countries: Home and Foreign. We will use r_H and r_F to denote the autarky equilibrium values of the relative prices (equal to the rate of return on investment) in the two countries. Now, suppose that $r_H > r_F$. That is, the relative price of present consumption is higher in Home than in Foreign. Following the logic

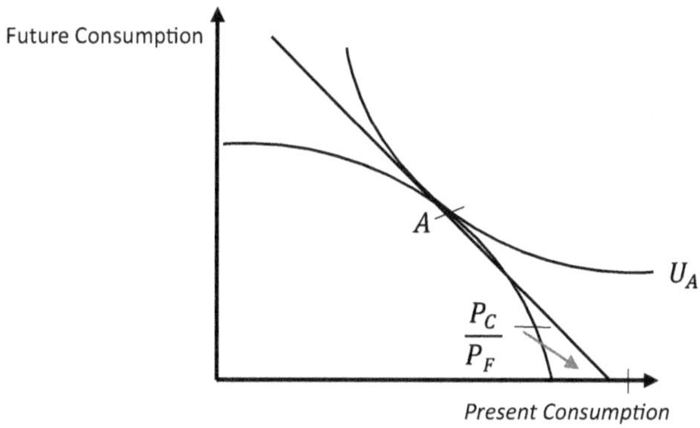

Figure 5.2: International borrowing and lending.

of comparative advantage developed earlier, it means that Home has a comparative advantage in future consumption and Foreign has a comparative advantage in present consumption. Therefore, Home should be importing present consumption and exporting future consumption. In other words, Home should be a borrower and Foreign should be a lender. As discussed earlier, this also implies that Home runs a trade deficit, while Foreign runs a trade surplus. Another way to say the same thing is that since the returns are higher in Home than in Foreign, capital will flow from Foreign to Home.

In the above discussion, we simply assumed that $r_{\mathrm{H}} > r_{\mathrm{F}}$. But what determines whether a country is a borrower or a lender in the international capital market? Here, we discuss two alternative determinants of international borrowing/lending.

(1) **Different investment opportunities:** Suppose that individuals in Home and Foreign have identical preferences between present consumption and future consumption. However, investment opportunities differ between the two countries. In particular, Home has better investment opportunities than Foreign. This would mean that Home's PPF is biased toward future consumption. Since the preferences are identical, the tangency between the PPF and the indifference curve in Home will be to the northwest of that in Foreign as shown in Figure 5.3. As a

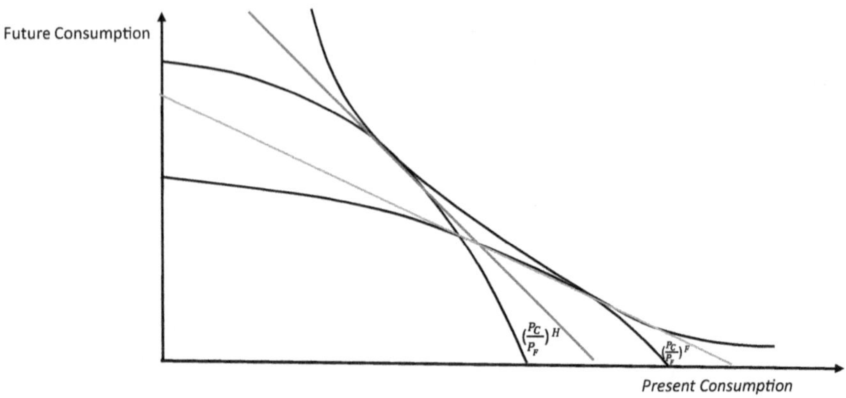

Figure 5.3: International borrowing and lending: different investment opportunities.

result, the slope of the common tangent in Home is steeper than that in Foreign: $r_{\mathrm{H}} > r_{\mathrm{F}}$.

(2) **Different preferences between present consumption and future consumption:** Suppose that Home and Foreign have identical investment opportunities leading to identical PPFs. However, Home consumers are more impatient; as a result, they want to consume more now and save less for each relative price. The result is that the indifference curve of Home will intersect the indifference curve of Foreign from below. As a consequence, the point of tangency for Home will be to the southeast of that in Foreign as shown in Figure 5.4. Again, the common tangent in Home is steeper than the common tangent in Foreign: $r_{\mathrm{H}} > r_{\mathrm{F}}$.

Therefore, a country can be an international borrower either because it has better investment opportunities or because its consumers have a stronger preference for present consumption.

The gains from intertemporal trade are similar to the gains from international trade in a model of comparative advantage. As shown in the Heckscher–Ohlin model, both countries will gain from trade by moving to a higher indifference curve compared to autarky. To see this, note from the discussion above that $r_{\mathrm{H}} > r_{\mathrm{F}}$. Now, when capital flows from Foreign to Home in response to higher returns there, the

Figure 5.4: International borrowing and lending: different preferences.

returns will be equalized in a fashion similar to the equalization of relative prices in models of comparative advantage. Therefore, the world rate of interest (or the relative price of present consumption), denoted by r_W, will settle between r_H and r_F. At the new relative price, which is steeper than the autarky relative price in Foreign and flatter than the autarky relative price in Home, both countries will gain by reaching a higher indifference curve as in the Heckscher–Ohlin model.

The model discussed above does a good job of capturing international capital flows in the form of portfolio investment such as buying stocks or bonds in a foreign country by individuals or institutions or lending to foreign firms by financial institutions. However, there is another kind of capital movement called FDI, which has a different underlying cause to which we turn next.

5.4 Foreign Direct Investment

FDI is undertaken by multinational firms which acquire a controlling stake in a foreign business. At the outset, we can distinguish between Greenfield FDI and mergers & acquisitions. In the case of Greenfield FDI, a multinational firm sets up a new plant or business in a Foreign country. For example, if Tesla motors sets up a new factory in China, it is an example of Greenfield FDI. If an American multinational firm acquires a Chinese company, it is called mergers and acquisitions. Sometimes, people use the term "Brownfield" FDI to refer to cases where a multinational firm enters into a joint venture with a foreign firm.

There are two key motives for multinationality or FDI:

(1) To sell its product in a foreign market (Horizontal FDI).
(2) To buy/produce some inputs in a foreign market (Vertical FDI).

5.4.1 *OLI framework of John Dunning (mainly for horizontal FDI)*

Economist John Dunning has developed the "OLI framework" to study multinational firms.[4] O refers to ownership, L refers to location and I refers to internalization.

- **Ownership:** In order to become a multinational enterprise (MNE), a firm must have an asset that it wants to exploit in a foreign market. Examples of assets are brand name, blueprint, business practices, etc. Once a firm has decided that it wants to exploit its asset by selling in a foreign market, it has to make the location decision.
- **Location:** This refers to a firm's decision on whether to produce the good in the Home market and export or to produce it in the Foreign market.

What determines the location decision of a firm? One can think of two things here: production cost and trading cost. If the production cost is lower in the host country, then the multinational firm would prefer to locate its production facility in the host country rather than export. Alternatively, even if the production cost is lower in the

[4]Dunning, J. H. (1977). Trade, location of economic activity and the MNE: A search for an eclectic approach. In Ohlin, B. Per-Ove Hesselborn, and Per Magnus Wijkman, eds., *The International Allocation of Economic Activity*. London: Macmillan.

MNE's parent country, because of the high trading cost, it may make sense for the MNE to locate its production facility in the host country.

When talking about the location decision, it is worth mentioning the proximity–concentration trade-off that firms face in situations where there are fixed costs involved in production, which give rise to economies of scale. To keep things simple, assume that the production process involves a fixed cost and a constant marginal cost. Now, the MNE already has a plant in its parent country, so it only has to incur the marginal cost of production for exports plus the trading cost. But, if it wants to produce in the host country, it has to incur the fixed cost of setting up a plant and then the marginal cost of production. Therefore, if the fixed cost of setting up a plant is high, then the firm will concentrate its production in the single plant in its parent country. Alternatively, if the trading cost is very high, then it will set up a plant in the host country. This trade-off is known as the proximity–concentration trade-off.

Now, suppose that the multinational has decided to locate the production facility in the host country. It has one more decision to make and that is where the internalization comes into play.

- **Internalization:** This has to do with the decision of whether to keep production internal to the firm boundary or license the technology to an outside producer for a license fee. That is, internalization refers to factors affecting the choice between licensing and FDI. If the firm keeps production within the firm boundary, then it is engaging in FDI. Licensing involves the transfer of technology from the MNE to a local firm. If the transfer of technology is difficult, then the MNE would prefer to go the FDI route. For example, McKinsey, a consulting firm, has its business practices embodied in its consultants, and therefore it would be very difficult for McKinsey to transfer technology and its preferred route is FDI. Licensing also involves a contract between the MNE and the local firm. Anything that makes contracting difficult is going to favor FDI over licensing.

Having discussed the economics behind horizontal FDI, we turn to vertical FDI.

5.4.2 *Vertical multinationality*

In this case, a multinational firm wants to obtain some inputs from a foreign country. The decision that the firm has to make is whether to buy inputs from a foreign supplier by entering into a contract or to set up a plant in the host country to produce the input within its firm boundary. For example, suppose that General Motors wants to get steering wheels for its automobiles from Mexico. General Motors has two options: enter into a contract with a Mexican producer of steering wheels or set up a plant in Mexico to produce steering wheels. The former is called offshore outsourcing and the latter is called FDI. The two together are called offshoring. In the Industrial Organization literature, this decision is also called the "make vs buy" decision. "Make" is making the input within the firm boundary and "buy" is buying the input from an outside party.

How does a firm decide whether to engage in offshore outsourcing or FDI? If the input is something that can be bought off the shelf, then the firm is more likely to engage in offshore outsourcing. However, most of the inputs that firms use are customized and therefore cannot be bought off the shelf. In this case, offshore outsourcing involves a contract between the input-using firm in one country and the input-supplying firm located in a foreign country. There are transaction costs associated with writing, negotiating and enforcing contracts. If these transaction costs are high, then the FDI route is preferred over offshore outsourcing.

Since FDI is a result of the profit-maximizing choice of firms, it lowers the cost of serving the foreign market for a multinational firm in the case of horizontal FDI. This leads to lower prices for consumers in the host country and increases the profitability of the MNE. In the case of vertical MNE, the cost of producing goods is lower for the MNE because it can obtain inputs at a lower cost from abroad as compared to procuring it domestically. This lower cost results in lower prices for consumers and higher profits for the firm. These are the sources of gain from FDI. In addition to these gains, many times, the activities of multinational firms lead to technology transfers either directly or through spillover effects in the host countries. These are sources of additional gains from FDI for host countries.

5.5 Concluding Remarks

While much of this book focuses on international trade in goods, movements of factors of production are an important facet of globalization. This chapter provided a brief discussion on the economics behind the movements of labor and capital across international borders. It also discussed the welfare implications of these factor flows.

Problem Set

Question 1

Look at the table below giving the production function in a hypothetical country.

# of workers	Total Output	Marginal Output	Average Output
1	200		
2	370		
3	520		
4	660		
5	780		
6	890		
7	995		
8	1090		
9	1170		
10	1220		

a) Complete the columns for marginal output and average output. Now, suppose there are two countries with 2 factors of production labor and capital. Each country has a fixed amount capital and labor.

b) Suppose Home is capital abundant and has only 2 units of labor, while Foreign is labor abundant and has 8 units of labor. Calculate the rewards of labor and capital in each country.
c) Now, suppose the two countries open their borders to migration. Which is going to be the host country for migration and which is going to be the source country? How many workers are going to migrate?
d) Calculate the impact of migration on the following: (i) wages of native workers in the host country; (ii) wages of workers left behind in the source country; (iii) impact on capital owners in the host country; (iv) impact on capital owners in the source country; and (v) world output.
e) In light of the answer to part (d) above, state who is going to oppose migration and who is going to support it.
f) If you were a policymaker interested in maximizing world output, would you support or oppose migration?

Question 2

Provide 2 reasons why migration can benefit source countries.

Question 3

Look at the balance of payment account of your country. Does your country run a trade deficit or a trade surplus? Is your country an international borrower or a lender? Have things changed in the last few years? If yes, then explain by looking at the savings and investment data for your country what the cause of change in trade balance is.

Question 4

We discussed 2 reasons why a country could run a trade deficit and hence be an international borrower. In which of these 2 cases should one be worried about the sustainability of the deficit and the ability of the country to pay back foreign loans in the future?

Question 5

Suppose the US government increases the tariffs on cars imported from Germany. How would this affect the decision of BMW regarding exporting cars to the US vs undertaking FDI to produce cars in the US?

Chapter 6

Commercial Policy

6.1 Introduction

In this chapter, we study the welfare implications of instruments of commercial policy. Commercial policy refers to policies to intervene in trade. Examples include tariffs, quotas, export subsidies and export taxes. We first develop a framework to study the welfare implications and then study specific policies.

Unlike in the models of comparative advantage where welfare was measured by the utility level of a representative individual, and utility itself was a function of many goods, here, we develop a framework for studying welfare in a partial equilibrium setting. That is, we look at welfare by focusing on one good at a time.

In the partial framework, we will measure welfare in a market by adding consumer surplus, producer surplus and government revenue. Consumer surplus is simply the difference between the price that a consumer is willing to pay and the price that the consumer actually pays. Geometrically, it is going to be the area below the demand curve and above the price line. Producer surplus is the difference between the price that a producer actually gets and the minimum price that the producer is willing to sell the good for. Geometrically, it is going to be the area above the supply curve and below the price line. Finally, if policy intervention results in revenue generation, then we add the revenue to our measure of welfare. The implicit assumption is that the revenue is given back to consumers in a lump-sum fashion or used to generate public goods that everyone benefits from. If the policy results in the government making a payment, as will be the case when we study export subsidies, then we subtract it from the measure of welfare. Therefore,

$$\text{Welfare} = \text{consumer surplus} + \text{producer surplus} + \text{government revenue.}$$

In the discussion of commercial policy, we make a distinction between the small-country case and the large-country case. The small-country case is one where the country is too small to affect the world price of the good in question. Therefore, any policy intervention by this country will leave the world price unaffected. The large-country case is one where the country is large enough to affect the world price. If a large country intervenes in trade, it will change the world price and we will have to take that into account when studying the welfare implications of commercial policy.

Before studying the welfare implications of commercial policies, let us study the gains from trade using our partial equilibrium framework.

6.2 Gains from Trade

Suppose that the good in question in steel, and a country's demand and supply curves are shown in Figure 6.1. The market price in the absence of trade (autarky, hereafter) is obtained by the interaction of demand and supply curves and is given by P^*. The welfare in autarky is simply the sum of the consumer surplus (area ABC) and the producer surplus (area BCE). Now, suppose that the country can freely trade in steel in the world market. The world price of steel is given by P_{W}, which is less than the autarky price of P^*. Since steel is cheaper in the world market, the country will import steel. The situation with free trade in steel is shown in Figure 6.1.

The amount of steel imported is the gap between the demand curve and the supply curve at the world price of P_{W} and is given by FG. The welfare with free trade is again the sum of consumer surplus (area AGD) and producer surplus (area DEF). We can verify that the

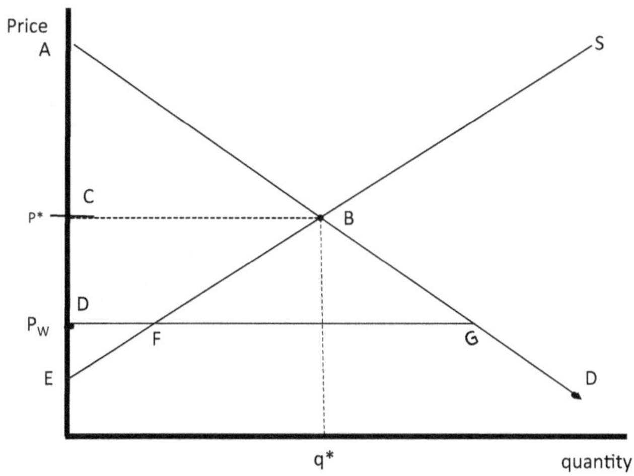

Figure 6.1: Gains from trade.

sum of the producer and consumer surplus in the case of free trade (area AGFE) is larger than in autarky (area ABFE). The difference is the triangle (area BFG), which captures the gains from trade. Note that the consumer surplus is larger than in the autarky case, whereas the producer surplus is smaller. However, the gain of consumers is larger than the loss of producers, resulting in an overall welfare gain.

Gain in welfare from free trade:

$$\text{Change in consumer surplus} = +\text{BCDG}$$

$$\text{Change in producer surplus} = -\text{CBFD}$$

$$\text{Change in welfare} = +\text{BFG}.$$

Now, we are ready to study the welfare implications of commercial policy instruments. The first policy we study is the tariff for a small-country case.

6.3 Tariffs in a Small Country

Starting from a free trade situation, we can study the welfare implications of tariff in a small country. A tariff is basically a tax

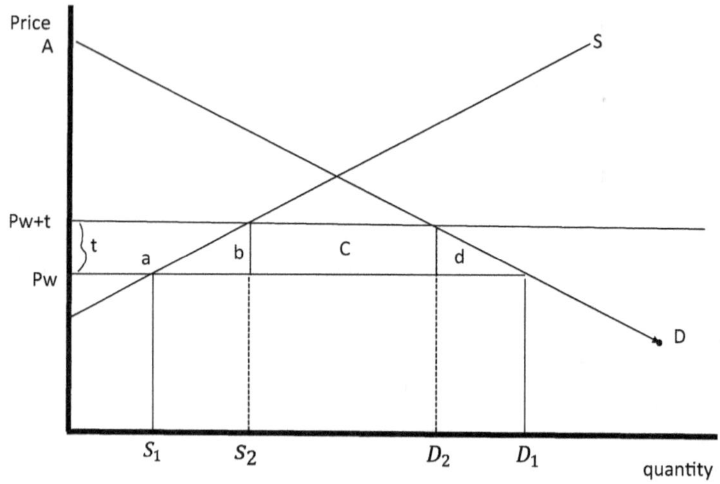

Figure 6.2: Welfare implications of a tariff.

on imports. To fix ideas, suppose that the world price of steel is \$500 per ton and the government imposes a tariff of 10%. This will increase the effective domestic price to \$550. When a tariff is a percentage of the price, it is called *ad valorem* tariff. Alternatively, a tariff can be per unit of a good, say \$50 per ton of steel. In this case also, the domestic price will rise to \$550 per ton. Therefore, an *ad valorem* tariff of 10% is equivalent to a per unit tariff of \$50. Most tariffs happen to be *ad valorem*, but it is easier to draw pictures for the per unit case, so we will work with per unit tariffs in this chapter. The impact of a tariff is shown in Figure 6.2.

In Figure 6.2, P_{w} is the world price of the good at which the country produces S_1 and consumes D_1. As a result, the free trade level of import M equals $D_1 - S_1$. Now, when the country imposes a tariff of t per unit of the good, the domestic price becomes $P_{\mathrm{w}} + t$. We can find the change in welfare resulting from the tariff compared to the free trade situation by adding the change in consumer surplus, the change in producer surplus and the change in government revenue or tariff revenue. We have seen how to calculate changes in the consumer and producer surplus. The change in tariff revenue is simply the tariff revenue because the tariff revenue in the free trade situation is zero. Since the amount of imports is $M = D_1 - S_1$, and there is a tariff of

t per unit of imports, the tariff revenue is simply $t \times M$. Note from Figure 6.2 that

$$\text{Change in consumer surplus} = -\,(a + b + c + d),$$

$$\text{Change in producer surplus} = +\,a,$$

$$\text{Change in tariff revenue} = +t \times M = c,$$

$$\text{Change in welfare} = -b - d.$$

That is, the change in welfare as a result of a tariff is negative and the welfare loss equals two small triangles b and d. The loss of welfare given by triangle b is called the production distortion because a tariff distorts the domestic production compared to the free trade situation. The level of production in the free trade situation is S_1, but the tariff distorts it to S_2. Similarly, the triangle d is called the consumption distortion because in the free trade situation, the consumption was D_1 but now it has been distorted to D_2. So, a tariff distorts production upward and consumption downward relative to the free trade situation. The two distortions together are called the "deadweight loss". Note that the total consumer surplus loss is $a + b + c + d$; however, a part of it, area a, is a transfer to producers. Similarly, a part, area c, comes back to consumers through tariff revenue. However, the areas b and d are not recouped by the country. Therefore, they constitute a "deadweight loss" from the country's point of view.

Next, we turn our attention to the tariff in the large-country case.

6.4 Tariffs in a Large Country

As mentioned earlier, the difference between a small country and a large county is that the tariff in a large country will affect the world price. How will the world price be affected by the tariff in a large country? First of all, the world price of a good will be determined by the world demand for the good, and the world supply of the good as is shown in Figure 6.3.

In Figure 6.3, D_1 is the initial world demand for the good and S_1 is the initial world supply. This results in a world price of P_1. Now,

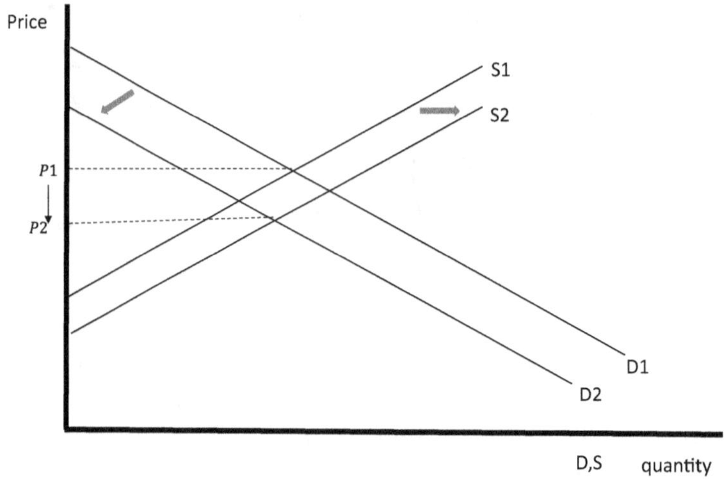

Figure 6.3: Impact of a tariff on world price.

when a large country imposes a tariff, it affects the world demand and supply. How does it affect them? We can understand that from the small-country case discussed earlier. We saw that when a small country imposed a tariff, it raised the domestic price of the good, which increased the domestic supply of the good and reduced the domestic demand for it. However, these changes in the small country were too insignificant to affect the world price. The changes in the large country will increase the world supply of the good and reduce the world demand for it. That is, at each world price, the supply in the large country is more than in the free trade case because the tariff-ridden price in the large country is higher. Similarly, the demand in the large country is lower at each world price than in the free trade case. As a consequence, the world supply curve shifts to the right to S_2 and the world demand curve shifts to the left to D_2. This, in turn, leads to a decrease in the world price of the good to P_2. That is, a tariff imposed by a large country reduces the world price of the good.

Having understood the impact of a tariff imposed by a large country on the world price, we can study the welfare implications of a tariff. The welfare implications are shown in Figure 6.4.

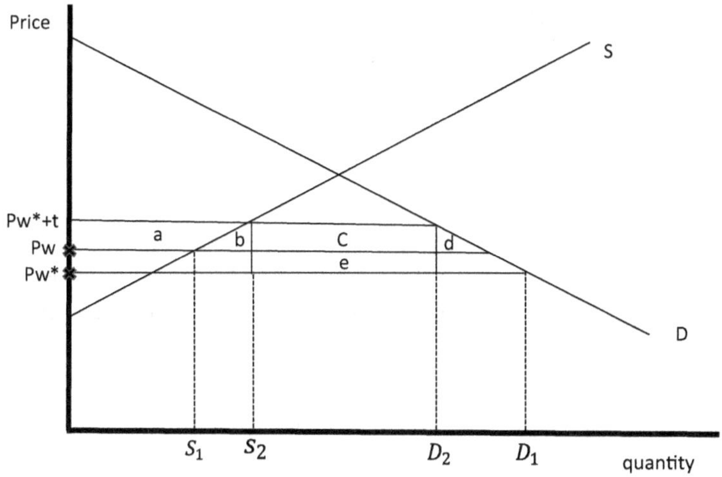

Figure 6.4: Impact of tariff on welfare in the large country case.

As shown in Figure 6.2, we start with a free trade equilibrium with a world price of P_{w}. Now, when a large country imposes a tariff of t, the world price decreases to P_{w}^* through the mechanism discussed earlier. As a result, the tariff-ridden price in the importing country is $P_{\mathrm{w}}^* + t$, which is less than $P_{\mathrm{w}} + t$ because $P_{\mathrm{w}}^* < P_{\mathrm{w}}$. Now, the changes in consumer surplus, producer surplus and tariff revenue from Figure 6.4 are as follows:

$$\begin{aligned}\text{Change in consumer surplus} &= -(a + b + c + d),\\ \text{Change in producer surplus} &= +a,\\ \text{Change in tariff revenue} &= +t \times M = c + e,\\ \text{Change in welfare} &= e - (b + d).\end{aligned}$$

The key difference from Figure 6.2 is that the tariff revenue is $c + e$ and as a result the change in welfare has a positive term e. The triangles b and d are production and consumption distortions, respectively, as shown in Figure 6.2. But the positive term e captures the "terms of trade effect" of a tariff, which merits some additional discussion.

The terms of trade refer to the terms at which a country trades in the international market. Generally, this is expressed as the ratio of the price of exports to the price of imports. If this ratio increases, then it is said that a country's terms of trade have improved because it gets more for its exports relative to what it has to pay for its imports. The ratio can increase either because the price of exports has increased or because the price of imports has decreased. To see this clearly, suppose that there is an increase in the world price of oil. How does this affect the terms of trade of different countries? If a country is an exporter of oil, its terms of trade have improved. If it is an oil importer, its terms of trade have worsened. Since we are in a partial equilibrium framework looking at one good at a time, a decrease in the world price of the imported good is a terms of trade improvement and a decrease in the world price of the exported good is a worsening of the terms of trade.

Having explained the meaning of terms of trade, we can clearly see that a decrease in the world price of the imported good caused by the tariff in the large country is an improvement in its terms of trade. Area e in Figure 6.4 captures this improvement. Note that area e equals $(P_{\mathrm{W}} - P^*_{\mathrm{W}})M_2$, where M_2 is the level of imports after the imposition of a tariff and $P_{\mathrm{W}} - P^*_{\mathrm{W}}$ is the decrease in the world price of the imported good. Therefore, what is the impact of a tariff on welfare in the large-country case? From the expression for the change in welfare derived earlier, we see that welfare increases if $e > b + d$ and welfare decreases if $e > b + d$. That is, the change in welfare can be positive or negative. Starting from a free trade situation, it can be mathematically shown that a small tariff improves welfare. When the tariff is small, the terms of trade effect, e, dominates the distortions $(b + d)$; as a result, welfare increases. Once the tariff becomes sufficiently large, the distortions start dominating the terms of trade effect, and hence welfare starts decreasing. There is a level of tariff, t_{o}, that maximizes welfare in a large country. This is known as the optimal tariff. This is shown in Figure 6.5 where welfare is maximized at t_{o}.

If the tariff is very high, say more than t_{p}, it chokes off imports completely and the welfare of the country is back to the autarky

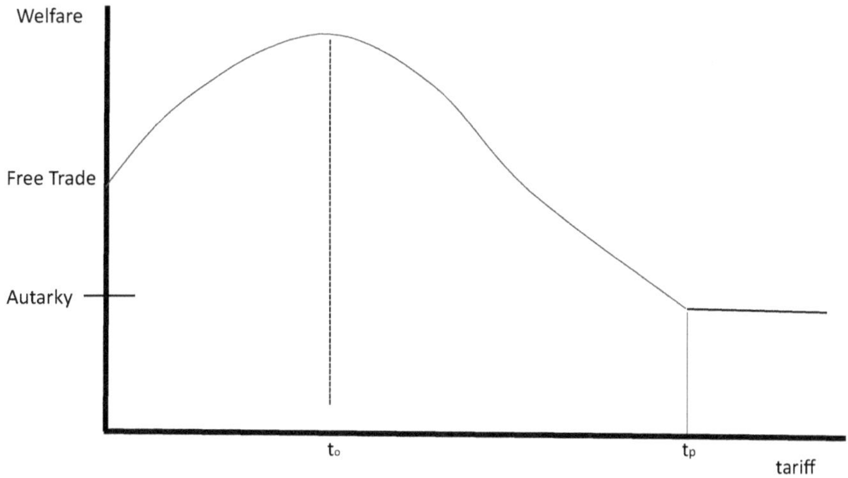

Figure 6.5: Optimal tariff for a large country.

level. The level of tariff, t_{p}, at which imports become zero, is called the prohibitive tariff.

According to the *Economist*, August 8, 2019, the steel tariff of 25% imposed by the Trump administration in 2018 initially increased the price for the US producers from \$600 to \$800 per ton, but increased capacity building and higher production brought the price back to pre-tariff levels by the summer of 2019. Since the US is a large country, an increase in the supply of steel induced by the steel tariff reduced the world price of steel.

Next, we discuss the implications of quantitative restrictions.

6.5 Quantitative Restrictions

Quantitative restrictions refer to policies restricting the quantity of a good that can be traded. For example, the US government, instead of imposing a tariff of 10% on steel can simply restrict the import of steel to a certain amount, say 500 million tons. We are going to discuss the welfare implications of two types of quantitative restrictions: a purely domestic quota (or simply quota) and a voluntary export restraint (VER). In the former case, the importing country's government unilaterally imposes a quantitative

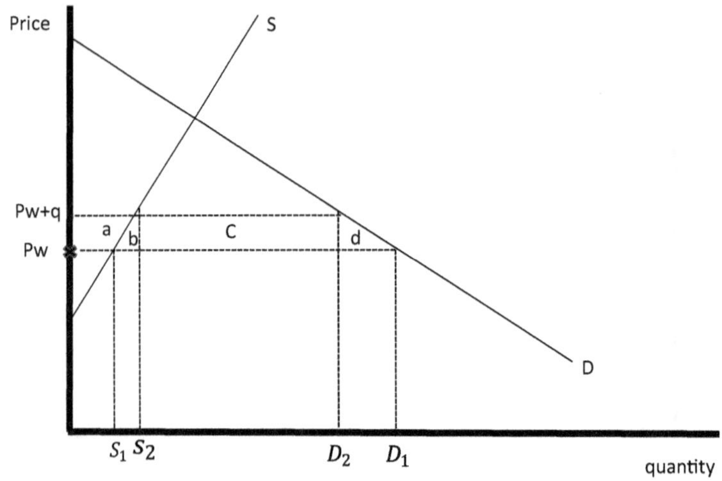

Figure 6.6: Impact of a quota.

restriction, while in the latter case it negotiates with the exporting country so that the exporting country agrees to restrict the export to a certain amount. We discuss the welfare implications of both these types of quantitative restrictions. However, we only discuss the small-country case. In the large-country case, there will be a terms of trade effect similar to that of a tariff.

6.5.1 *Welfare implications of a domestic quota*

Sticking to the steel example, suppose that the world price of steel is P_{w}. With free trade, the amount of steel imported would have been M_1 $(D_1 - S_1)$ as shown in Figure 6.6. Now, suppose the government says that the amount of steel imported cannot exceed some amount $M_2 < M_1$. Since at the free trade price of \$500 the amount imported was M_1, restricting the import to $M_2 < M_1$ is going to create a shortage of steel in the country, which will raise the domestic price to $P_{\mathrm{w}} + q$, where q is the quota rent per ton of steel. Note that at the price of $P_{\mathrm{w}} + q$, the demand for steel is D_2 and the supply is S_2 so that $M_2 = D_2 - S_2$.

To complete the welfare analysis, we need to discuss who gets the quota rent. It is clear that the consumers pay a price of $P_{\mathrm{w}} + q$

and domestic producers get a price of $P_{\mathrm{w}} + q$ for every ton of steel they produce and sell. The traders who import steel buy steel from the world market at a price of P_{w}, but sell it in the domestic market at a price $P_{\mathrm{w}} + q$. The question is how is it decided who can import steel. The government in the country has a couple of options in terms of distributing the license for importing steel in the amount of M_2. The government can either auction licenses, in which case it can raise revenue of q per ton of steel or total revenue of $q \cdot M_2$. Alternatively, it can simply give the licenses on a first-come-first-served basis, in which case the traders who are lucky enough to get the licenses will keep the quota rent of $q \cdot M_2$. In both cases, this money stays in the economy, so it will be added to the measure of welfare in a fashion similar to the tariff revenue.

It is clear from Figure 6.6 that the welfare impact of a purely domestic quota is very similar to that of a tariff. In Figure 6.6, the change in welfare compared to the free trade situation is exactly equal to $-(b + d)$. The only difference is that the tariff revenue of c is replaced by the quota rent of c. Therefore, a quota causes production and consumption distortions similar to a tariff. Therefore, the welfare implications are very similar to that of a tariff. In fact, if we compare a tariff, t, that results in an import of M_2 and a quota that restricts the import to M_2, the welfare implications are identical. The quota will lead to a quota rent per unit of the good of q which must equal t. Therefore, the tariff revenue of t^*M_2 is replaced by an equivalent quota rent of q^*M_2, leaving the welfare exactly the same in the two cases.

It must be mentioned that the result on the equivalence between a tariff and a quota holds only if the domestic market is perfectly competitive, which is what we have assumed. If the market is imperfectly competitive, it is possible that a quota leads to greater welfare losses than an equivalent tariff.

Next, we turn to the welfare implications of a VER.

6.5.2 *Welfare implications of a VER*

As mentioned earlier, in the case of a VER, it is the exporting country that restricts its export to a certain amount. Therefore, for example, in Figure 6.6, the free trade level of import is M_1. This is also the export of some country to the importing country. Now, instead of the importing country unilaterally restricting imports to $M_2 < M_1$, it is the exporting country that restricts the export to M_2. Thus, now the exporting country has to issue export licenses. Since the shortage of the good is going to raise the price to $P_w + q$ again, it is the exporters that keep the VER rent of q per unit of the good. Again, parallel to the domestic quota case, the exporting country can either auction the export licenses and raise revenue or give the export licenses on a first-come-first-served basis. In either case, the rent goes to the exporting country. Therefore, the welfare implications of a VER are as follows. The change in welfare from the importing country's point of view is simply the sum of changes in consumer and producer surplus, which amounts to $-(b + c + d)$. That is, the welfare losses are much larger compared to a domestic quota $(b + c + d > b + d)$ because the quota rent goes to the exporting country. This raises an obvious question. Why would a country ever use a VER rather than a quota to restrict imports? Some history is useful here.

The first well-known use of a VER was by the US to restrict the import of Japanese cars to the US market. The US domestic car manufacturers — Ford, GM and Chrysler — used to make big cars which were not very fuel efficient. This was not much of an issue for the US car buyers as long as fuel was cheap. But, in the 1970s, there were two oil shocks (1973 and 1979) when the Organization of Petroleum Exporting Countries (OPEC) decided to hike the price of oil. When the oil prices jumped, American car buyers suddenly started caring about the fuel economy of their cars. The Japanese car manufacturers were good at making small, fuel-efficient cars. Suddenly, there was a surge of import of Japanese cars to the US and US car manufacturers were in trouble. That is when they asked the Reagan administration for help. And, help came in the form of a VER agreement with Japan whereby Japan agreed to restrict the export of cars to the US. The main reason for going the VER route rather than a unilateral quota was to prevent retaliation. That is, if the US had imposed a unilateral quota on Japanese cars, Japan could have retaliated by creating barriers to the import of the US goods in the Japanese market, leading to a trade war and potentially much greater welfare losses. Therefore, a negotiated VER route was preferable to a unilateral quota.

Next, we discuss a policy intervention on the export side called export subsidies.

6.6 Export Subsidies in a Small Country

In an attempt to promote exports, countries subsidize their exporters. It works in the following way. Suppose that the world price of cheese is $5 per pound. Now, if the French government gives an export subsidy to cheese producers of $0.50 per pound, the French exporters of cheese will collect $5.50 per pound of cheese exported, where $5 comes from the world market and $0.50 from the government. This is what would happen if the country giving export subsidies was small and could not affect the world price. If the country is large, the world price will also be affected, which we will discuss in Section 6.7.

In discussing the welfare implications of export subsidies, we also need to discuss what happens to the domestic price. If a French farmer can get $5.50 per pound from exporting, would they want to sell for anything less than $5.50 in the French market? The answer is clearly no. Does that mean the price will rise to $5.50 in the French market? We will assume this to be the case. Keep in mind that in order for this to work, the French government should be able to prevent the export of cheese by other foreign producers to the French market at the world price of $5 per pound. That is, implicitly the French government is backing the French cheese producers not only by giving them an export subsidy but also by ensuring that the domestic price in France is $5.50.

Now, we can see the welfare implication of an export subsidy in Figure 6.7.

In Figure 6.7, P_W is the world price of the good. Note that in order for the country to be an exporter, the world price must be greater than the domestic price that would be obtained in the absence of trade, which is the case in Figure 6.7 because the world price is above

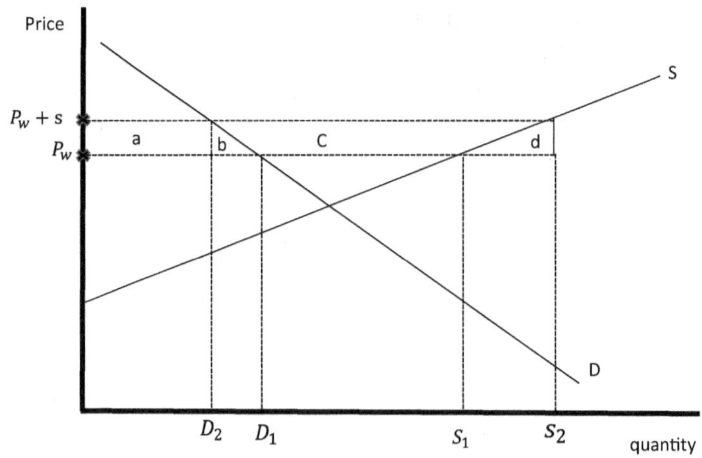

Figure 6.7: Impact of an export subsidy for a small country.

the intersection of the demand and supply curves. At the world price, the country would export $X_1 = S_1 - D_1$ amount of the good. Now, when the government announces an export subsidy of s per unit of the good, the price rises in the Home market to $P_{\mathrm{w}} + s$. At this price, the producers produce S_2, but consumers demand only D_2; hence, $X_2 = S_2 - D_2$ is the export. The change in welfare is as follows:

$$\text{Change in consumer surplus} = -(a + b),$$

$$\text{Change in producer surplus} = +(a + b + c),$$

$$\text{Change in government revenue} = -(b + c + d),$$

$$\text{Change in welfare} = -(b + d).$$

Compared to the tariff case, the new term is the change in government revenue, which is simply the amount of export subsidy given by the government. This is equal to $s \cdot X_2$, where s is the subsidy per unit and X_2 is the amount exported. The change in welfare is negative and involves the production distortion, triangle b, and consumption distortion, triangle, d. The two together are called the "deadweight loss". Therefore, an export subsidy for a small country causes welfare losses similar to a tariff.

Next, we discuss the large-country case.

6.7 Export Subsidies in a Large Country

The difference in the large-country case is going to come from a change in the world price. And, the change in the world price is similar to that for a tariff. Recall from the small-country case that when a small country grants an export subsidy, the supply increases from S_1 to S_2 and the demand decreases from D_1 to D_2. Therefore, the change in the world price can again be captured by Figure 6.3 where the world supply shifts to the right and the world demand shifts to the left. As a result, the world price falls. The welfare implications for the large country are captured in Figure 6.8.

In Figure 6.8, the initial world price is P_{w}. When a large country grants an export subsidy, the world price of the good declines to P_{w}^*. As a result, the price that producers get, and the price faced by domestic consumers, is $P_{\mathrm{w}}^* + s$. The change in welfare is given as follows:

$$\text{Change in consumer surplus} = -(a + b),$$

$$\text{Change in producer surplus} = +(a + b + c),$$

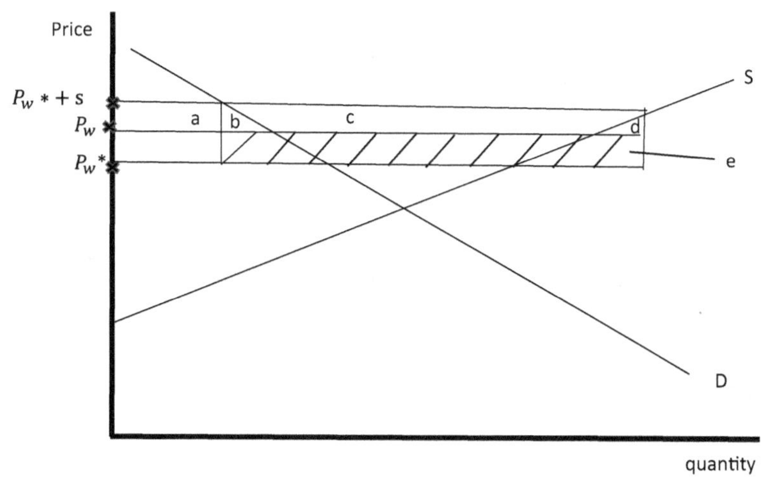

Figure 6.8: Impact of an export subsidy for a large country.

$$\text{Change in government revenue} = -(b + c + d + e),$$

$$\text{Change in welfare} = -(b + d + e).$$

Two terms need explanation here. The export subsidy in Figure 6.8 is the area $(b+c+d+e)$ because the amount of export is X_2 and the subsidy per unit of s is the gap between P^*_W+s and P^*_W. Given this, the welfare loss is not just the production and consumption distortions, b and d, respectively, but also the area e. The area e is the terms of trade loss for the country. We had discussed the terms of trade gain from a tariff for a large country. There, a decrease in the price of the good that the country was importing was a terms of trade gain. Here, a decrease in the price of the good that the country is exporting is a terms of trade loss. Therefore, the welfare implications of an export subsidy for a large country are worse than that in a small country. The country also suffers a terms of trade loss in addition to suffering production and consumption distortion.

Before concluding this chapter, we quickly discuss a couple of trade policy interventions that are always in the headlines.

6.8 Anti-Dumping Duties and Countervailing Duties

We discussed the economics of dumping in Chapter 4. Now, when a foreign firm is implicated in a dumping case, the government in the Home country is allowed to impose a tariff, which is called the anti-dumping duty. For example, suppose that a Chinese manufacturer is found to be dumping solar panels in the US market. Suppose that the fair value of the panels is deemed to be \$1000 and the Chinese firm in question sells it at \$800. Then, the US government can impose an anti-dumping duty of \$200 per panel. This will raise the price of Chinese solar panels in the US to \$1000. As far as the welfare implications are concerned, they are exactly like those of a tariff because at the end of the day, an anti-dumping duty is a tariff.

A countervailing duty is a tariff imposed to offset the export subsidies given by a foreign government. Now, suppose that in the earlier example of the solar panels, the Chinese manufacturer receives an export subsidy from its government of \$200 per panels. That is, whenever it exports a panel to the US, it collects \$800 from the US consumers and \$200 from the Chinese government in the form of an export subsidy. In this case, the WTO rules allow the US government to impose a tariff of \$200 per panel to offset the export subsidies. Again, this will raise the price of Chinese solar panels in the US to \$1000. The welfare implications will be exactly the same as in the case of a tariff discussed earlier.

Therefore, from the welfare point of view, both anti-dumping duties and countervailing duties are just a tariff by a different name.

6.9 Concluding Remarks

Countries use a number of commercial policy instruments to restrict or promote trade. Instruments like tariffs, quotas and VERs restrict the import of a good. Export subsidies, on the contrary, promote the export of a good. Our welfare analysis of these policies revealed that for a small country, all these interventions cause welfare losses. For a large country, a tariff yields terms of trade gains, and hence there is a possibility of a welfare improvement if the country sets the tariff at the optimal level. However, the optimal tariff argument runs into a problem if the exporting country retaliates by imposing a tariff as well. We study this issue in detail in Chapter 7.

Problem Set

Question 1 (tariff, quota, VER, in the small country case)

Suppose the demand curve in Laos for coffee is

$$D = 300 - 5P$$

The supply curve is

$$S = -50 + 5P$$

a) Calculate the equilibrium price and quantity of coffee when Laos is in autarky.

Now, suppose Laos is a small country, and hence unable to affect the world price of coffee. The world price of coffee is \$25 per bag.

b) Determine the free trade equilibrium values of the following variables: amount produced domestically, amount consumed, amount imported, and the price at which it imports coffee.

Now, suppose Laos imposes a tariff of \$5 per bag on imported coffee.

c) Determine the values of the following variables: amount produced domestically, amount consumed, amount imported, the price of coffee in Laos, tariff revenue, consumption distortion loss, production distortion loss, and total welfare loss. Show the results diagrammatically.

Suppose instead of a tariff, the government decides to use a quantitative restriction. It imposes a quota of 70 bags and auctions the quota license to the highest bidder.

d) Determine the values of the following variables: amount produced domestically, amount consumed, amount imported, the price of coffee in Laos, revenue raised from quota auctions, consumption distortion loss, production distortion loss, and total welfare loss. Show the results diagrammatically.

Now, suppose that instead of a quota, the government of Laos enters into a Voluntary Export Restraint (VER), whereby the government of Indonesia (which is the exporter of coffee to Laos) agrees to restrict the export of coffee to 70 bags.

e) How would the results in part d) change? Is the welfare of Laos higher in the case of a quota or a VER?

Question 2 (tariff in the 2-country case)

Home's demand and supply curves for coffee are

$$D = 110 - 20P; \quad S = 10 + 20P$$

Foreign's demand and supply curves for coffee are

$$D^* = 90 - 20P; \quad S^* = 30 + 20P$$

a) Derive (numerically) and graph Home's import demand schedule and Foreign's export supply schedule. What are the autarky equilibrium prices and quantities in the two countries?
b) Now, allow Foreign and Home to trade with each other. Find and graph the equilibrium under free trade. What is the world price of coffee? What is the volume of trade?

Now, suppose Home imposes a specific tariff of 1 on coffee imports.

c) Determine (numerically) and graph the effects of the tariff on the following: (1) the world price of coffee; (2) the price of coffee in Home; (3) the price of coffee in Foreign; and (4) the volume of trade in coffee
d) Calculate and show graphically the terms of trade gain, the efficiency loss, and the total effect on welfare in Home of the tariff.

Question 3 (Export subsidy in a small country)

Suppose Ethiopia's demand and supply curves for coffee are

$$D^* = 90 - 20P; \quad S^* = 30 + 20P$$

a) Find the autarky equilibrium price of coffee and the quantity bought and sold in Ethiopia.
b) Now, suppose the world price of coffee is 2 and Ethiopia is a small country which cannot affect the world price of coffee. If Ethiopia opens up to trade and practices free trade in coffee, what is going to be the price of coffee in Ethiopia? How much coffee will Ethiopia export?

c) Calculate the impact of opening to trade on the welfare of Ethiopia. Show your results diagrammatically.
d) Now, suppose Ethiopia decides to subsidize the export of coffee. In particular, it gives an export subsidy of 0.5. What happens to the domestic price of coffee in Ethiopia?
e) With the export subsidy of 0.5, what happens to the production, consumption, and export of coffee in Ethiopia?
f) Calculate the welfare implications of an export subsidy of 0.5 compared to the free trade situation.

Question 4 (Export subsidy in the 2-country case)

Assume that the market for soybeans is competitive. The demand for soybeans from users in China is given by the demand curve Q = 90 – P, and the supply of soybeans from Chinese producers is given by the supply curve Q = P – 20. China buys soybeans from Brazil. The demand and supply curves for soybeans in Brazil are given by Q = 40 – P and Q = P – 10.

a) What would be the price of soybeans in China and how much soybeans are bought and sold in the absence of trade?
b) What would be the price of soybeans in Brazil and how much soybeans are bought and sold in the absence of trade?
c) Now, calculate the import demand schedule for China and the export supply schedule for Brazil. Suppose Brazil and China trade freely in soybeans. Calculate the world price of soybeans and the amount traded.
d) Calculate the impact of free trade on the welfare of Brazil compared to autarky.
e) Now, suppose Brazil gives an export subsidy of 4. Calculate the new world price of soybeans and the volume traded. What happens to the terms of trade for Brazil?
f) Calculate the impact of export subsidy on the welfare of Brazil compared to the free situation. Show your results graphically.

Chapter 7

Arguments for and Against Intervention in Trade

7.1 Introduction

In Chapter 6, we studied the welfare implications of various types of trade policies. In earlier chapters, we also studied how gains from trade arise in various theoretical models of international trade. Using all this information, we first look at some arguments for and against intervention in trade. In Chapter 8, we will look at the political economy of trade policy.

7.2 Arguments Against Intervention in Trade

Our theoretical models based on comparative advantage (Ricardian and Heckscher–Ohlin models) showed us that gains from trade arise because of the ability to import a good at a lower cost than procuring it domestically. The Krugman model (based on internal increasing returns to scale and love of variety) showed us that countries could gain from trade by having access to a larger number of varieties at lower prices. The gains from trade were also confirmed in Chapter 6 when we looked at one market at a time. There, we showed that, for a small country, free trade maximizes welfare (sum of producer and consumer surplus) and any intervention in trade causes consumption and production distortions. This constitutes the basic argument against intervention in trade.

7.3 Arguments for Intervention in Trade

Are there any arguments for intervention in trade? Now, we look at one somewhat robust argument and one non-robust argument for intervention in trade.

7.3.1 *Terms of trade argument for a large country*

In Chapter 6, we studied commercial policy for a small country as well as a large country. The difference was that a policy intervention in a small country could not affect the world price of the good, in question but intervention by a large country could. In particular, we saw that when a large country imposed a tariff, it reduced the world price of the good, which conferred a terms of trade gain on the large country imposing the tariff. Effectively, a large country has market power in international trade, which it can exploit to its advantage. Therefore, the welfare of a large country is higher with a tariff compared to the free trade situation. This is the essence of the terms of trade argument for intervention in trade, which gives rise to the "optimal tariff".

This is a sound theoretical argument for intervention in trade. However, it could lead to trouble in practice because in the real world, many countries can have market power and if they start using it simultaneously, it will result in a trade war without any terms of trade gains. To see this clearly, suppose there are only two large countries in the World: the US and China. China exports steel to the US and the US exports soybeans to China. Starting from a free trade situation, if the US imposes a small tariff on steel and China does not retaliate, it will improve the US terms of trade and consequently its welfare compared to the free trade situation. The same argument applies if China imposes a tariff on soybeans and the US does not retaliate. However, starting from a free trade situation, if both the US and China impose a tariff (the former on steel and the latter on soybeans), then the terms of trade do not improve for either and the tariff in each country causes production and consumption distortions. The terms of trade from the US point of view refer to the price of soybeans relative to the price of steel. A US tariff without Chinese retaliation will reduce the relative price of steel, which is an improvement in the US terms of trade. The opposite is true for a Chinese tariff on soybeans. That is, it will reduce the price of soybeans relative to steel, which is the same as an increase in the price of steel relative to soybeans. Therefore, a mutual tariff nullifies the terms of gains by each importer. What this example also makes clear is that, unlike the gains from trade based on comparative advantage or love of variety, the terms of trade gains for a country come at the cost of its trading partner. That is, the US terms of trade gain in our example is a terms of trade loss for China, and this is the reason why a tariff is likely to invite retaliation. Given this, economists generally advocate against using tariffs for terms of trade reasons.

Next, we look at the domestic market failure based argument.

7.3.2 *Domestic market failure based argument*

It is commonly asserted that there may be a case for intervention in trade if there is domestic market failure. To understand this argument, we first need to clarify what we mean by market failure. Market failures refer to situations where a market left to its own devices does not maximize social welfare measured by the sum of consumer and producer surplus. If the markets are imperfectly competitive (say monopoly or oligopoly), then it is quite likely that the social welfare is not maximized. However, even if the market is perfectly competitive, market failures can occur because of the presence of externalities on the production or consumption side.

Externalities are benefits or losses that are experienced from the production or consumption of a good by agents who are not the producers or consumers of the good. The classic case of a negative externality is the air pollution created from the smoke emitted by a factory, which affects everyone living nearby adversely. Suppose that the factory produces steel which is sold outside the town in which the factory is located. In this case, the air pollution created by the factory is an externality for the residents of the town. A consequence of the externality in this example is that the marginal social cost of producing a ton of steel by this factory exceeds the marginal private cost incurred by the factory owners. This is because the factory owners do not take into account the negative externality that they are creating for the residents of the town. If the steel industry is competitive, then the amount of steel produced is determined by the condition price = marginal cost. The marginal cost here is the marginal private cost, which is less than the marginal social cost because of the externality. If there are no externalities on the consumption side, then the price of steel which reflects the marginal private benefit from consuming a ton of steel will correspond to the marginal social benefit. Therefore, marginal private benefit ($\equiv$ Price) = marginal social benefit (MSB) = marginal private cost ($\equiv$ MC) $<$ marginal social cost (MSC). That is, we have MSB $<$ MSC, which implies that there is too much production of steel from the society's point of view. Generally, whenever MSB $\neq$ MSC, there is market failure and the social welfare is not maximized. In general, whenever the production of a good creates a negative externality, we have MSB $<$ MSC. On the contrary, if the consumption of a good confers positive externalities on others, then the market will be in a situation where MSB $<$ MSC, and so the market without any intervention underprovides this good.

Now, let us discuss trade policy in the presence of market failures. Suppose that the economy produces a good whose domestic production confers positive externalities on other agents. For example, the good in question could be a manufacturing good such as textiles the domestic production of which improves the technological capability of the country and allows improved production of other manufacturing goods. In terms of our example of market failure, the domestic production of this good confers a positive externality on other agents in the economy. Therefore, the marginal social benefit is higher than the marginal private benefit. For the discussion of policy, it is important to keep in mind that this extra benefit occurs if the good is produced domestically. It does not arise from the consumption of the good but from the production of the good.

Now, let us start with the free trade situation and then look at the impact of a small tariff. Suppose that the world price of the manufacturing good in question is P_{W}. For the free trade situation, social welfare is as shown in Figure 7.1.

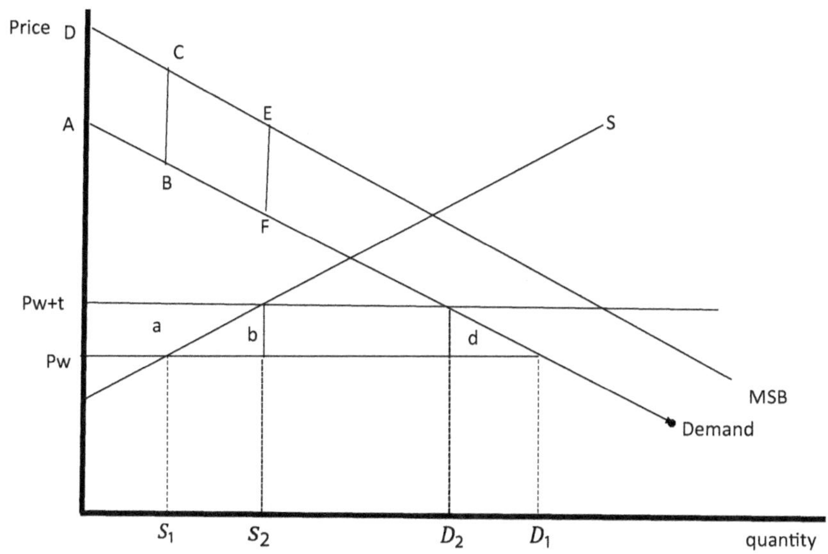

Figure 7.1: Domestic Market failure argument against free trade.

The demand curve captures the marginal private benefit and the curve lying above it, denoted by MSB, is the marginal social benefit curve. The gap between the two captures the extra social benefits arising from the externality. In the absence of externalities, welfare in the free trade situation is given by the sum of consumer surplus and producer surplus. The consumer surplus is the area below the demand curve and above the world price line, P_{W}, and the producer surplus is the area below the price line P_{W} and above the supply curve. Now, in the presence of externalities, the extra area ABCD is added to welfare. This area is the gap between the demand curve and the MSB curve to the left of quantity S_1, which is the domestic output in the free trade situation.

7.3.2.1 *Welfare effect of a tariff*

Now, suppose that the country imposes a small tariff of t. We will assume that this is a small country, so the world price is not affected. As a result, the domestic price is going to be $P_{\mathrm{W}} + t$. Ignoring the extra social benefits, the impact of this tariff on welfare is the same as that discussed in Chapter 6, so the welfare loss is given by the two triangles b and d, which are production and consumption distortions, respectively. Now, let us bring in the extra social benefits. The extra social benefits arise because the tariff has raised the domestic production from S_1 to S_2. This increases the social benefit by the area BCEF. Therefore, the overall impact of the tariff on welfare is BCEF $-(b+d)$, which can be positive if the tariff is chosen appropriately. Therefore, a tariff can potentially raise welfare compared to the free trade situation. This is the essence of the domestic market failure argument for intervention in trade.

Now, we are going to analyze the welfare effect of a production subsidy which raises the domestic output by the same amount.

7.3.2.2 *Welfare effect of a production subsidy*

Suppose that instead of imposing the tariff, the government offers a production subsidy. Furthermore, the amount of production subsidy is exactly the same as the amount of tariff. That is, production subsidy per unit of output is s, which is equal to t. While domestic producers receive a subsidy from the government, trade is free. If there are no barriers to trade, then the price in the country is going to be the same as the world price P_{W}. Therefore, consumers will continue to consume amount D1 that they consumed in the free trade situation. How much do domestic producers produce? For every unit they produce, they receive P_{W} from domestic consumers and s from the government, giving them a total price of $P_{\mathrm{W}}+s$, which equals the price of $P_{\mathrm{W}}+t$ that they received in the case of a tariff. Therefore, producers will produce amount S_2 that they produced in the case of a tariff. Thus, domestic production is the same in the case of a tariff and a production subsidy. However, domestic consumption is higher in the case of a production subsidy and is at the same level, D_1, as in the free trade case.

Now, let us do the welfare calculation compared to the free trade situation. Since consumers face the world price, there is no consumer surplus loss compared to the free trade situation. What about producer surplus? Since producers receive the same price as in the case of a tariff, their gain is the same as in the case of a tariff, which is area a in Figure 7.1. There is no tariff, so there is no tariff revenue. However, the government has to raise money to give production subsidy. Therefore, the government expenditure on subsidy enters the welfare calculation just as export subsidies did in Chapter 6. What is the amount of production subsidy? It is subsidy per unit of s times the domestic production S_2, which equals area $a + b$. Therefore, the sum of change in producer surplus and government subsidy is $-b$ (government subsidy exceeds the gain in producer surplus). The extra social benefit is the same as in the case of a tariff, which is given by BCEF. Therefore, the total change in welfare is BCEF $-b$.

Now, let us compare the change in welfare in the case of a tariff to the change in welfare in the case of a production subsidy. It is clear from the discussion above that BCEF $- b >$ BCEF $- (b + d)$. That is, the increase in welfare is greater with a production subsidy compared to an equivalent tariff. What we have shown is a very important insight in economics. If there is a domestic market failure, there is a domestic policy instrument such as a production subsidy which does better than a tariff.

Although market failures are common, economists believe that the domestic market failure argument for intervention in trade is flawed. A domestic market failure is always best treated at its source; it calls for domestic rather than trade intervention. In our example, the goal is to increase the domestic production of the good, which is better accomplished through a production subsidy than a tariff. A production subsidy does not raise the domestic price facing consumers above the world price, and hence does not cause any consumption distortion. A tariff causes a consumption distortion, and therefore is an inferior, second-best policy to offset domestic market failures. A tariff is indirectly a combination of a production subsidy and a consumption tax. It is the consumption tax component that causes unnecessary welfare loss that can be avoided by using a direct policy of production subsidy.

Similarly, if there are problems in the labor market, an employment subsidy may be better than a tariff. Furthermore, market failures are often difficult to analyze well enough to be sure about the appropriate policy recommendation. Because of difficulties in translating complex economic analyzes into real policies, free trade is considered a useful rule of thumb.

7.4 Concluding Remarks

In this chapter, we looked at the arguments for and against intervention in trade. The key argument against the intervention is that free trade provides welfare gains for a small country that will be reversed if the country tries to intervene in trade. This was amply demonstrated through welfare calculations for different commercial policy instruments in Chapter 6. Then, we looked at two arguments for intervention in trade: a terms of trade based argument and a domestic market failure based argument. We argued against the terms of trade based argument for intervention in trade because it is likely to attract retaliation from trading partners, which will nullify any terms of trade gains. The domestic market failure based argument is more sophisticated; however, even there, the conclusion was that the first-best policy is a domestic policy tool which can tackle the market failure directly. Trade intervention is at most a second-best policy: something that should be resorted to only if the domestic policy tool is not available for some reason. Given all this, economists tend to favor free trade as a matter of general principle.

Problem Set

Question 1

Suppose the demand and supply curves for computer chips in Botswana are given by the following equations:

$$\mathrm{D} = 300 - 5\mathrm{P}; \quad \mathrm{S} = -50 + 5\mathrm{P}$$

In addition, the production of each unit of computer chips yields extra social benefits of 15, which are not reflected in the demand curve. Also assume that the world price of computer chips is 20.

a) Calculate the total effect on welfare of a tariff of 10 per unit levied on imports. Show your results diagrammatically. {Remember to include the additional welfare from extra social benefits of 15 in your calculations.}
b) Now, suppose the government decides to give a production subsidy of 10 per unit instead of a tariff. Calculate the total effect of a production subsidy of 10 per unit on welfare. Show your results diagrammatically. {Remember to include the additional welfare from extra social benefits of 15 in your calculations.}
c) Why does the production subsidy produce a greater gain in welfare than the tariff?

Question 2

In this chapter, you looked at two arguments for intervening in trade: a terms of trade argument and domestic market failure-based argument. Which of these is a robust reason for intervening in trade?

Question 3

What is the main difference between the impact of a tariff on a small country and the impact on a large country?

Chapter 8

Political Economy of Trade Policy

8.1 Introduction

In Chapter 6, we studied the welfare implications of various trade policies. We saw that at least for a small open economy, trade restrictions led to welfare losses. For a large country, there was a terms of trade argument for restricting trade, but in Chapter 7 we argued that if trading partners start retaliating, then no country will get the terms of trade benefits of a tariff. Essentially, terms of trade changes are a zero-sum game: A country's terms of trade improvement is its partner's terms of trade loss. Given all this, most economists agree that free trade is a good policy default. However, we see pervasive trade restrictions in the real world. In the US, the Trump administration has used a variety of trade restrictions directed at various trade partners. In this chapter, we want to get a better understanding of how policies are made in democracies, which will help us understand trade policies better.

One key theme running through this chapter is that we can see a policy in place that benefits a handful of individuals even if it causes welfare losses to a large number of people. To set the stage, let us look at some numbers from the tariffs imposed by the Trump administration on washing machines. According to a report in the *New York Times* (April 21, 2019, https://nyti.ms/2Xvbwph), economists found that the tariff caused a consumer surplus loss of \$1.542 billion. If we assume that there are 300 million consumers in the US, the consumer surplus loss translates into a loss of approximately \$5 per consumer. The tariff revenue was a mere \$82 million. However, domestic producers clearly gain from a tariff. Since the creation of domestic jobs is touted as a benefit of the tariff, the researchers calculated that about 1800 new jobs were created due to these tariffs. The cost of each of these jobs was approximately \$817,000. That is, each of these new jobs was created at a cost of \$817,000 to consumers. In other words, the policy is an extremely inefficient way to create 1800 extra jobs. In addition to the lucky few workers who got a job producing washing machines, the real beneficiaries were the domestic washing machine manufacturers, mainly Whirlpool, which had brought the complaint in the first place. So, in general, domestic manufacturers (and some workers employed in those industries) gain from a trade policy intervention while consumers lose. This raises an obvious question: Why do we see a policy that causes welfare losses for 300 million consumers but benefits a handful of businesses and workers? The answer takes us into the realm of political economy.

The starting point of the political economy models is that actual policies are not necessarily arrived at by maximizing the aggregate welfare of the society. Instead, they may reflect the desires of individuals and groups who stand to gain a lot from a policy rather than national welfare that gets reflected in the objectives of governments.

How do the preferences of individuals get added up to produce the trade policy that we actually see? Various political economy models come up with different answers to this question. We discuss a few of them here. The first model we discuss is called the Median voter model.

8.2 The Median Voter Model

This model is applicable to democracies where governments are elected by a majority voting. To understand this model, suppose that there are two political parties, D and R, that are running in an election to come to power. To simplify things further, suppose that the only issue that voters care about is trade policy. Each voter has a preferred trade policy position and the voter will vote for the party whose trade policy position is closest to the voter's preferred trade policy. For example, suppose that a voter, let us call her voter-1, is a free trader, and hence her preferred trade policy is a tariff of zero. Now, suppose that party R announces that if it comes to power, it will enact a tariff of 10%. Similarly, party D announces that if it comes to power, it will enact a tariff of 25%. Which party will voter-1 vote for? The answer is R because the voter's preferred trade policy position of zero tariffs is closer to a tariff of 10% than 25%. Similarly, suppose another voter, voter-100, believes that trade with foreign countries is a bad idea. This voter would like a complete ban on trade. Clearly, this voter's policy preference is closer to party D's policy platform of 25% tariff than party R. So, voter-100 will vote for party R.

Now, suppose that the total number of voters in the country is N. We can order these voters according to their preferred policy position. Suppose that the lowest possible tariff that a voter wants is t_{min} and the highest possible tariff that a voter wants is t_{max}. We call the voter that wants t_{min} voter-1 and the voter that wants t_{max} voter-N. What is going to be very important for the results is a level of tariff t_{med} such that half the voters want a tariff greater than t_{med} and half the voters want a tariff less than t_{med}. The voter who wants a tariff of t_{med} is called the Median voter. Next, we argue that the policy position of both parties is going to converge to t_{med}. That is, in order to win a majority of votes, each party is going to announce a tariff of t_{med}. This is the Median voter result which we prove heuristically below.

To make things concrete, suppose that $t_{\text{med}} = 15\%$. That is, the Median voter prefers a tariff of 15%. Now, sticking to our earlier numbers for party R, suppose that party R announces a tariff of 5%. To beat party R, party D has an easy policy choice. Party D can simply announce a tariff of slightly higher than 5%, say 6%, and party D will get a majority of votes. How is this possible? Recall that $t_{\text{med}} = 15\%$. Thus, half the voters want a tariff of 15% or more. Therefore, when R announces a tariff of 5% and D announces a tariff of 6%, D easily wins a majority. We can repeat the same exercise for a tariff announced by D. That is, suppose that D announces a tariff of 25%. Now, R can announce a tariff of 24% and win a majority of votes because 50% of voters want a tariff of less than 15%. Therefore, for any tariff, t, announced by one of the two parties, the other party can undercut it by announcing a tariff of $t + \varepsilon$, where ε is a very small number, if $t < t_{\text{med}} = 15\%$. Similarly, if $t > t_{\text{med}} = 15\%$, then the other party can undercut it by announcing a tariff of $t+\varepsilon$. Thus, if each party wants to get a majority of votes, and does not want to be undercut by the other party, the only option they have is to announce a tariff of $t_{\text{med}} = 15\%$. If a party announces a tariff of 15%, the other party cannot undercut it by announcing a higher or lower tariff. If both parties use this reasoning, they will both end up announcing a tariff of 15%. In this case, it is not clear which party will win. But, that does not matter as far as the policy is concerned because whichever party comes to power will implement $t = 15\%$.

If the policies in democracies were made according to the Median voter model, they would reflect the preferred policy position of the voter in the middle. How good a job does the Median voter do of explaining trade policies? Unfortunately, the answer is not very good. As we saw in the washing machine tariff example, only a handful of people gain from the tariff on washing machines, while almost everyone else loses. So, if people were motivated solely by their economic gains/losses, they would not vote for a policy like a tariff on washing machines that causes welfare losses for 300 million consumers.

Next, we turn to the logic of collective action of Mancur Olson to understand trade policy.

8.3 Logic of Collective Action (Mancur Olson)

The economist Mancur Olson in his book *The Logic of Collective Action* argued that economic policies are like public goods where it is difficult to exclude anyone from getting the benefits of a policy.[1] Note that a public good is characterized by two features: non-excludability

[1]Olson, M. (1965). The logic of collective action. Harvard University Press, Cambridge.

and non-rivalry. Non-excludability means that it is very difficult to exclude anyone from benefiting from the good, while non-rivalry means that the consumption of the good by one person does not reduce the amount left for others. Sunlight would be a perfect example of a public good. Trade policy has both these features. For example, if the tariff on washing machines is reduced to zero, all consumers of washing machines benefit from it. It is hard to see how someone residing in the US could be excluded from benefiting from the lower price of washing machines. It is non-rival as well because when I benefit from the lower price of a machine, it does not reduce the benefit for anyone else. A problem with the provision of public goods is that it gives rise to the free-rider problem. That is, since no person can be excluded from benefiting from a lower price of the washing machine, instead of engaging in activism demanding the repeal of tariffs on washing machines, people may just enjoy leisure and hope that other people's activism leads to the policy change that they will benefit from. That is, the collective action that is required for the repeal of washing machine tariffs suffers from the free-rider problem.

Mancur Olson argued that smaller groups can overcome the collective action problem by getting organized. For example, since there are only a handful of washing machine producers, they can get organized more easily and solve the free-rider problem compared to the consumers of washing machine who are 300 million in the US. Furthermore, while each producer of washing machine has a lot to gain from a tariff on washing machines, each consumer loses only about $5 as we saw earlier. Given this, it may not be worthwhile for an individual consumer to lobby against tariffs on washing machines. On the contrary, producers can easily get organized and hire lobbyists to lobby on their behalf. Therefore, the logic of collective action predicts that we may see trade policies which favor a small group with large gains for each member of the group while the losers are numerous but lose only a small amount each.

While Olson's logic of collective action does a good job of explaining why we may see policies in place that benefit only a handful of people and cause losses for a large number of others, it does not exactly tell us how organized groups influence policies.

Recent models of political economy based on campaign contributions or political contributions provide a possible answer. Now, we discuss a more recent model of political economy — the Grossman–Helpman model — that sheds light on the channel of influence used by the organized interest groups.

8.4 The Grossman–Helpman Model

In a very influential paper titled "Protection for Sale" (*American Economic Review*, 1994), two famous economists, Gene Grossman and Elhanan Helpman, wrote down a theoretical model that clearly shows how the organized interest groups influence policy. The protection in the title of the paper refers to tariffs that aim to protect the domestic industry. In the model, there is a policymaker who not only cares about the aggregate welfare but also likes to get contributions from the organized interest groups. The contributions could take the form of campaign contributions or political contributions or could even be bribes. The reason why policymakers care for contributions in a western democracy where outright bribery is difficult is because they need money for running election campaigns, advertising their policy positions, etc. There is a trade-off facing a policymaker who cares about remaining in office or getting reelected. While popular policies maximizing general welfare attract votes, policies favoring special interest groups attract contributions that make it easier to run campaigns.

Grossman and Helpman posit an objective function for the policymaker, which is a weighted average of the general welfare and the contributions. Organized interest groups offer contributions to the policymakers which are contingent on the policy. It is like an organized interest group telling the policymaker that if you promise to impose a tariff of t, we will offer you a contribution of $c(t)$, where $c'(t) > 0$. That is, the contribution is an increasing function of the tariff. Therefore, if the policymaker promises a higher tariff, she can expect a larger contribution. Now, there are many organized interest groups and each is trying to influence the policymaker. In particular, it is possible that there are some lobbies for exporters as well, say in the US case lobbies for farmers exporting soybeans, who would like less protection or more free trade. More precisely, Grossman and Helpman model the policymaking process as an auction where different organized interest groups bid for protection, and more protection goes to higher bidders. It is as if protection is for sale, and hence the title of their paper. The key result of their theoretical model is that organized interest groups get positive protection or positive tariffs. The level of tariffs is inversely related to the elasticity of demand for imports. This captures the fact that the policymaker also cares about general welfare, and a tariff is more distortionary from the general welfare point of view the larger the elasticity of import demand. Finally, the tariff is increasing in the weight the policymaker puts on contributions and decreasing in the weight the policymaker puts on general welfare.

8.5 Empirical Evidence on the Influence of Lobbies on Trade Policy

There have been several empirical studies documenting the influence of lobbies on trade policy. Here, we are going to discuss one study by two economists Robert Baldwin and Chris Magee, titled "Is trade policy for sale? Congressional voting on recent trade bills", (*Public Choice*, 2000). They studied the voting patterns in the US house of representatives on two important trade policy-related issues and how the voting of the representatives was affected by contributions from lobbies. The two policies in question were a vote on approving the North American Free Trade Agreement (NAFTA) in 1993 and the Uruguay round of GATT negotiations in 1994. A YES would be support for free trade, while a NO would mean a policy stance against free trade.

They collected data on the contributions from lobbies representing labor and business interest groups. It is generally believed that at that time labor was against these trade agreements, while businesses were in favor of it. Therefore, the contribution from labor would have tried to persuade a representative to vote NO, while the contribution from businesses would have persuaded them to vote YES.

Table 8.1: Empirical evidence on lobbying and trade policy.

	Vote for NAFTA (1993)	**Vote for GATT (1994)**
Actual	229	283
Predicted	227	285
Without labor contribution	294	342
Without business contribution	186	250
Without any contribution	252	317
Effect of labor contributions	–67	–67
Effect of business contributions	41	35
Effect of total contributions	–25	–32

Source: Baldwin and Magee, *Public Choice* (2000).

Table 8.1 shows the actual results of the voting as well as the results of the empirical exercise.

The first row of the table shows the actual vote and since there are 435 house members, the numbers imply that both the agreements got more than enough YES votes to pass. The second row shows the prediction from the empirical exercise where Baldwin and Magee tried to predict the voting behavior of a representative based on the characteristics of their district as well as the contributions, if any, received from labor and business. The predicted numbers are very close to the actual numbers, suggesting that their empirical model did a good job of explaining the voting behavior of the representatives. The next three rows present the results of the counterfactual exercise. The row labeled "without labor contribution" shows the predicted votes if labor had not contributed but capital had contributed. In this case, there would have been 294 YES votes on NAFTA and 342 YES votes on GATT. The next row presents the numbers from the counterfactual exercise when labor contributed but business did not. The following row presents the results of the counterfactual exercise when neither labor nor business contributed.

The last three rows report the results on the effectiveness contributions in swaying the votes. When we compare the numbers for the row "without any contribution" with the row "without business contribution", the difference tells us the "effect of labor contribution". Looking at NAFTA, we can conclude that the contribution from labor was successful in persuading 67 representatives to vote NO on NAFTA while they would have voted YES without any contributions. The number for GATT was also 67. Similarly, comparing the row "without any contribution" with the row "without labor contribution" tells us the importance of business contribution, which was successful in persuading 41 members to vote on NAFTA and 35 members to vote on GATT while they would have voted NO in the absence of any contributions. Since both labor and business contributed, some of their contributions offset each other. In particular, on net, labor contribution was able to persuade 25 representatives to vote NO on NAFTA and 32 members to vote NO on GATT. Note that the numbers do not exactly add up because the true estimates are in fractions, but in the table we have used whole numbers. Overall, this empirical exercise clearly shows the influence of contributions on policy.

8.6 Concluding Remarks

The usage of commercial policy instruments like tariffs, quotas and export subsidies is pervasive across the world. In Chapter 6, we showed that these trade interventions cause aggregate welfare losses. This raised the obvious question of why we see such policies in place. This chapter answered that question using models of political economy of policymaking. The chapter also provided some empirical evidence consistent with the political economy models that show how organized interest groups influence policies that benefit a small group of producers but cause welfare losses for a large number of consumers.

Problem Set

Question 1

The United States government imposes restrictions on the import of sugar (which mainly takes the form VERs), which costs every consumer of sugar in the US about $6 every year. The policy benefits a handful of sugar producers in the US. Can the Median Voter model explain the restrictions on trade in sugar? Explain.

Question 2

You learnt in chapter 6 that a tariff reduces welfare (at least for a small country). Why do we still see countries using tariffs to protect domestic industry? Which of the political economy models you learned in this chapter best describes the actual trade policies?

Question 3

Suppose we look at 2 import-competing industries A and B in a large country like the United States. Suppose industry A has only a handful of firms and is geographically concentrated, while industry B has a large number of firms spread all over the US. Which of the 2 industries is more likely to get protection? Why?

Chapter 9

Preferential Trade Agreements

9.1 Introduction

Preferential trade agreements (PTAs) are agreements between groups of countries that liberalize trade within the group but keep trade barriers intact against countries from outside the group. In most cases, countries entering into a PTA reduce their mutual trade barriers to zero. Given our discussion of trade policy in Chapter 6 and the benefits of free trade throughout this book, it would seem that if a subset of countries mutually liberalize trade, it should improve the welfare of these countries. However, we are going to discuss that the answer is not so straightforward in a multi-country world. So, for example, if there are three countries in the world and two of them sign a PTA but keep trade barriers intact on the third country, it is possible for the welfare of the two PTA members to go down. When talking about PTAs, we will use the term member countries to refer to countries which form a PTA and non-member countries to refer to those which are not a part of the PTA. Before getting into a discussion on the welfare effects of PTAs, we first clarify a key difference between the two popular types of PTA: Customs Union and Free Trade Areas (FTAs).

9.2 Customs Union vs Free Trade Areas

A customs union is a PTA where member countries agree to have a common external tariff. That is, the tariff they impose on non-member countries must be the same. The European Union began as a customs union of six European countries after the treaty of Rome in 1957. These six member countries (France, Germany, Italy, Netherlands, Belgium and Luxembourg) agreed to have a common external tariff, meaning that they would have the same tariff on a non-member country like the United States or Japan. That is, France cannot have a tariff of 10% on Steel coming from the US while Germany has a tariff of 15%. Both must have exactly the same tariff on steel coming from the US.

An FTA is a PTA where member countries can choose to have their own external tariffs. An example of an FTA is the North American Free Trade Agreement (NAFTA) which has been renamed by the Trump administration as the US–Mexico–Canada Agreement (USMCA). Since USMCA is a free trade agreement, the US and Canada can decide to have different tariffs on automobiles coming from Germany or Japan.

In principle, FTAs are easier to agree upon because each country can have its own external tariffs and hence there is no need for protracted negotiations over what the common external tariff should be. However, FTAs present their own problems in enforcement or implementation. That is, in order to enforce an FTA, countries have to come up with complex "rules of origin" (ROO). ROO refer to what constitutes a good produced in a member country which will incur a zero tariff and what constitutes a good produced in non-member countries which will incur the relevant external tariff. To see why ROO are needed, suppose that the tariff on Japanese automobiles in Mexico is 15%, while the tariff in the US is 5%. Now, in the absence of ROO, a Japanese auto exporter will first export the car to the US because the US has a lower tariff and then reexport it to Mexico and try to pass off the car as a US-made car so that there are no Mexican tariffs on the car. This way, a Japanese car will avoid the higher 15% tariff in Mexico. The ROO will have to define what constitutes a

US-made car so that it can be sold without incurring a tariff in Mexico, in particular what percentage of the value of a car must be added within the FTA for it to qualify for zero tariffs.

The USMCA has a whole chapter (Chapter 4) devoted to explaining the ROO. The following is one provision of ROO:

> *A good will qualify as originating if the value of all non-originating materials used in its production that do not undergo an applicable change in tariff classification is not more than 10% of the transaction value or total cost of the good (provided the good satisfies all other applicable origin requirements). This de minimis threshold is currently 7% under the NAFTA.*

To see how pervasive PTAs are, the World Trade Organization (WTO) website (www.wto.org) lists a total of 242 FTAs and 21 customs unions at the time of writing this chapter in December, 2019.

Having described the two types of PTA, we next turn to the welfare implications of PTAs. The below discussion is in general terms so it will be applicable to both the customs unions and the FTAs.

9.3 Trade-Creating PTA

Suppose that there are three countries in the world: countries A, B and C. Countries A and B sign a PTA, so they are the member countries and country C is the non-member country. Let us think of a good, say shirts, that country A imports. The price that country A has to pay to import a shirt from country B is \$20, while the price that country A has to pay to import a shirt from country C is \$23. Now, suppose that before entering into a PTA, country A had identical tariffs on goods coming from countries B and C. Let us call this tariff, t, and in the shirt example think of this as a tariff of \$5 per shirt. Before the PTA, it is clear that the tariff-ridden price of a shirt coming from country B will be \$25 while that from country C will be \$28. Clearly, consumers would prefer to buy shirts from country B because it will be cheaper for them. What happens when country A enters into a PTA with country B? Now, country A eliminates tariffs on country B but keeps them intact on country C.

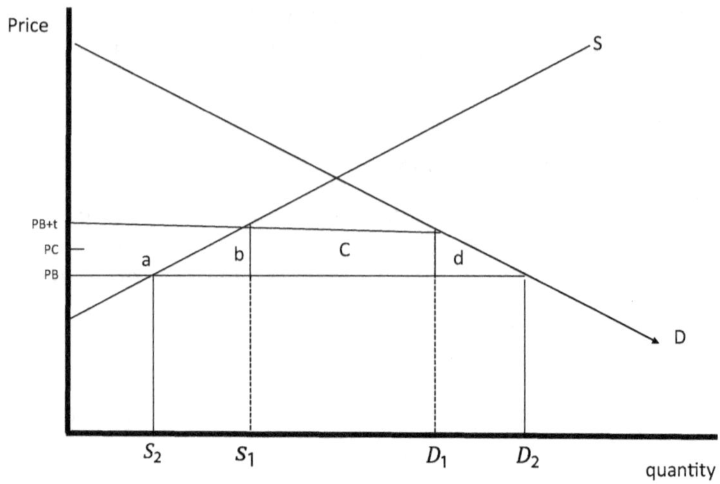

Figure 9.1: Trade creating PTA.

Therefore, the price of a shirt coming from B goes down to \$20 for consumers, but the price of a shirt coming from country C remains at \$28. In this case, consumers will keep buying shirts from country B. Moreover, the import of shirts from country B will increase because for consumers the price of a shirt has gone down from \$25 to \$20. The welfare implications are shown in Figure 9.1.

In Figure 9.1, P_{B} is the border price (before tariffs) of a shirt coming from country B and P_{C} is the border price of a shirt coming from country C. The tariff-inclusive prices in the pre-PTA situation are $P_{\mathrm{B}} + t$ and $P_{\mathrm{C}} + t$, respectively. Since $P_{\mathrm{B}} < P_{\mathrm{C}}$, it must be the case that $P_{\mathrm{B}} + t < P_{\mathrm{C}} + t$, and hence country A imports shirts from country B. In the pre-PTA situation, the amount of imports is $M_1 = D_1 - S_1$ and the welfare is going to equal the sum of consumer surplus, producer surplus and the tariff revenue. After the signing of the PTA, the shirts continue to be imported from country B, but the price that consumers pay goes down to P_{B} because the tariff on B goes to zero. As a result, the number of shirts imported from B goes up to $M_2 = D_2 - S_2$. It is easy to see that $M_2 > M_1$ and $M_2 - M_1$ is the amount of new trade that has been created in shirts. This is an example of "trade creation" induced by PTA, which is a source of welfare gain. To see the welfare implications, note that we are simply going from a tariff equilibrium with a tariff-ridden price of $P_{\mathrm{B}} + t$ to a no-tariff equilibrium with a price of P_B. Therefore, the changes in consumer surplus, producer surplus, tariff revenue and total welfare are as follows:

$$\text{Change in consumer surplus} = +(a+b+c+d),$$
$$\text{Change in producer surplus} = -a,$$
$$\text{Change in tariff revenue} = -c,$$
$$\text{Change in welfare} = +(b+d).$$

The welfare exercise above is the opposite of the welfare exercise we did for a tariff in the case of a small country. There, we showed that a tariff led to a welfare loss of areas b and d. Here, the country is going from a tariff equilibrium to a free trade equilibrium with a welfare gain of area $b+d$. Thus, we have shown that the PTA leads to more trade and an increase in welfare for member country A. The PTA in this case is a trade-creating PTA.

9.4 Trade-Diverting PTA

Next, we discuss what is called a trade-diverting PTA. To discuss this case, all we have to do is flip the prices of shirts coming from countries B and C. In the numerical example, suppose that the border price of a shirt coming from country B is \$23 and that coming from country C is \$20. Now in the pre-PTA situation, there is an identical tariff on both countries, so country A imports shirts from country C and the tariff-ridden price for consumers is \$25. This situation is shown in Figure 9.2.

The initial equilibrium is one with a price of $P_C + t$. In the post-PTA equilibrium, the price falls to P_B; as a result, the imports again increase from $M_1 = D_1 - S_1$ to $M_2 = D_2 - S_2$. The welfare implications are as follows:

$$\text{Change in consumer surplus} = +(a+b+c+d),$$
$$\text{Change in producer surplus} = -a,$$
$$\text{Change in tariff revenue} = -(c+e),$$
$$\text{Change in welfare} = +(b+d) - e.$$

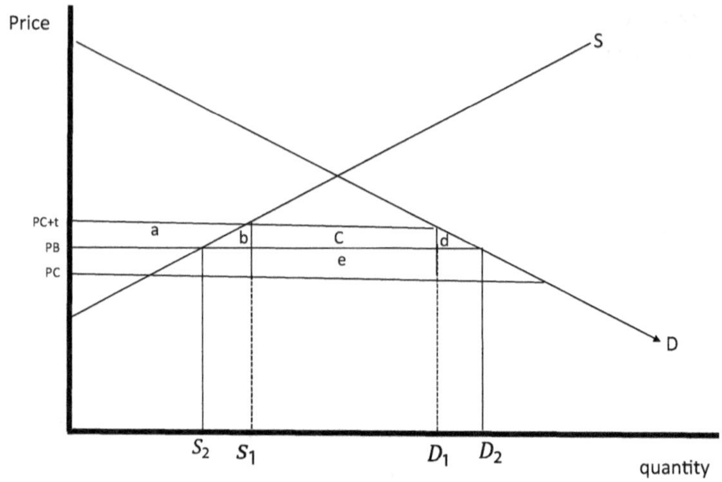

Figure 9.2: Trade diverting PTA.

Note that the change in welfare is ambiguous because we have two positive areas, b and d, and a negative area e. The key thing to note in the welfare analysis is that the tariff revenue declines by area $c+e$ because the volume of import was M_1, which incurred a tariff of t. What the PTA has done in this case is to divert the trade of shirts away from country C to country B. Note that the border price of shirts coming from country C is lower than that from country B, but because of discriminatory trade liberalization, country A switches its imports from the non-member country C to the member country B. This is what is called "trade diversion", which can potentially cause welfare losses. If the area e in the picture is greater than $b + d$, then the PTA causes welfare losses for country A.

The reason why country A may lose from a PTA is because it suffers terms of trade losses in the example in Figure 9.2. Recall that the terms of trade losses occur either because a country has to pay more for imports or because it gets less for exports. In our example, country A was paying a price of P_{C} for shirts before the PTA, but afterward it had to pay P_{B}, which is greater than P_{C}. The gap $P_{\mathrm{B}}-P_{\mathrm{C}}$ captures the terms of trade losses for country A. The total amount of loss is calculated as $(P_{\mathrm{B}} - P_{\mathrm{C}})M_1$ because in the pre-PTA situation, country A was importing M_1. Notice that this is exactly equal to area e. Therefore, compared to the pre-PTA situation, country A suffers a terms of trade loss in the amount of e, which is a source of welfare loss that must be balanced against the gains arising from the reductions in production and consumption distortion captured by areas b and d.

Overall, if a PTA creates a lot of trade as shown in Figure 9.1, then it is likely to be welfare improving, but if it causes a lot of trade diversion, as shown in Figure 9.2, then it can cause welfare losses.

9.5 Empirical Evidence

In a paper published in the *American Economic Review* in 2004,[1] Daniel Trefler estimated the trade-creating and trading-diverting effects of the US–Canada free trade agreement signed in 1988. He found evidence of both trade creation and trade diversion for Canada and concluded that trade creation exceeded trade diversion thereby yielding welfare gains for Canada. That is, there is evidence that Canada gained from the free trade agreement with the US.

In his study of NAFTA, reported in a paper published in the *Review of Economics and Statistics* in 2007, John Romalis found substantial evidence of trade diversion by the US in favor of Mexico after the signing of NAFTA.[2] That is, the US started importing goods from Mexico that it was previously importing from other countries. However, there was substantial trade creation as well. That is, the US increased the imports of goods from Mexico that it was already importing. He found that the overall welfare effect was a wash; that is, the positive welfare effect from trade creation was offset by the negative effect of trade diversion. Interestingly, he also found that Mexico suffered a small welfare loss, suggesting that the trade diversion effect slightly outweighed the trade creation effect for Mexico.

[1]Trefler, D. (2004). The long and short of the Canada-U.S. free trade agreement. *American Economic Review*, *94*(4): 870–895.
[2]Romalis, J. (2007). NAFTA's and CUSFTA's impact on international trade. *The Review of Economics and Statistics*, *89*(3): 416–435.

Problem Set

Question 1

Suppose the demand and supply curves for a bag of coffee in Laos are given by

$$D = 300 - 5P; \quad S = -50 + 5P$$

a) Assume that Laos imposes a tariff of $5 per bag of imported coffee to begin with. Laos can import coffee either from Brazil or Indonesia. The price of coffee from Indonesia is $20 per bag, while the price of coffee from Brazil is $25 per bag. Now, suppose Laos enters into a free trade agreement with Indonesia. First, calculate the impact of the free trade agreement on the volume of imports for Laos. Is this a trade-creating free trade agreement or a trade-diverting free trade agreement? Next, calculate the impact of the free trade agreement on the welfare of Laos. Show your results diagrammatically.

b) Assume again that Laos imposes a tariff of $5 per bag of imported coffee to begin with. The difference from part (a) is that the price of coffee from Brazil is $20 per bag, while the price of coffee from Indonesia is $25 per bag. Now, suppose Laos enters into a free trade agreement with Indonesia. Calculate the impact of the free trade agreement on the welfare of Laos. Show your results diagrammatically. Is this a trade-creating free trade agreement or a trade-diverting free trade agreement? What is the terms of trade gain or loss for Laos from entering into a free trade agreement with Indonesia?

Question 2

What is the main difference between a Customs Union and a Free Trade Area? Go to the World Wide Web and find 2 examples of Customs Union and 2 examples of Free Trade Area. Is your country a part of a Customs Union or a Free Trade Area? If yes, list them.

Chapter 10

The World Trade Organization

10.1 Introduction

The period 1870–1913 is considered to be the golden age of globalization when trade, capital flows and migration were all at very high levels relative to the world GDP. During the inter-war period (1919–1939), there was a reversal of globalization with countries erecting large barriers to trade. The egregious example of this was the Smoot–Hawley tariffs enacted in the US in 1930, which raised the average tariffs by roughly 20%, which prompted other countries to retaliate.

Toward the end of the Second World War, representatives from 44 countries met at the UN monetary and financial conference in Bretton Woods, New Hampshire, in July 1944, to discuss rebuilding Europe as well as issues such as high trade barriers and unstable exchange rates. The trade-related issues were formalized in 1947 and the General Agreement on Tariffs and Trade (GATT) was born with the purpose of reducing trade barriers and promoting free trade among member nations.[1]

[1]Visit https://www.wto.org/ for detailed history and features of GATT/WTO.

Table 10.1: GATT negotiations.

Rounds of GATT	% cut in tariffs	Average tariffs as a % of 1931 level
First round (Geneva, 1947)	21.1	52.7
Second round (Annecy, 1949)	1.9	51.7
Third round (Torquay 1950–1951)	3.0	50.1
Fourth round (Geneva 1955–1956)	3.5	48.9
Fifth Dillon round (Geneva, 1961–1962)	2.4	47.7
Sixth Kennedy round (Geneva, 1964–1967)	36	40.5
Seventh Tokyo round (Geneva, 1974–1979)	29.6	21.2
Eighth round (Uruguay, 1986–1994)	38.0	13.1
Ninth round (Doha, 2001–)		

Under the aegis of GATT, countries met periodically for negotiations on lowering trade barriers. These periodic negotiations became known as "rounds". Table 10.1 gives a summary of tariff cuts in each round of GATT negotiations and compares the average tariff to the level prevailing in 1931.

From Table 10.1, we see that a substantial amount of trade liberalization was achieved through various rounds of GATT negotiations. As a consequence, at the end of the Uruguay round, the average tariffs came down to 13% of the level in 1931. This has been accompanied by a massive growth in international trade since the end of the Second World War as we saw in Chapter 1 with the dramatic increase in the exports–GDP ratio for the world as a whole.

The Uruguay round, which began in 1986, was concluded in 1994, and at the end of this round it was decided to create a permanent body called the World Trade Organization (WTO) to oversee world trade. The WTO came into existence on January 1, 1995, and was headquartered in Geneva, Switzerland.

While GATT was just a set of rules for conducting trade, the WTO is a formal international institution governing an expanded set of global interactions including trade in services and intellectual property protections.

10.2 Key Provisions of GATT/WTO

10.2.1 *Most-Favored-Nation (MFN) clause: Article I of GATT*

This clause refers to the idea that every country belonging to GATT/WTO must be treated the same. That is, in general, a GATT member cannot discriminate against another GATT member. To fix ideas, suppose that India, France and Japan are three GATT/WTO members. Now, MFN means that India cannot have a tariff of 25% on automobiles coming from Japan and a tariff of 15% on automobiles coming from France. India should treat both Japan and France on equal terms and must have identical trade barriers against them. The issue of MFN used to be in the news every year in the US before China joined the WTO in the year 2001. Before China's entry into the WTO, the US had to decide whether to treat China on a par with the WTO members or discriminate against China. The US decided to grant China the MFN status, which effectively meant that China was treated on a par with other WTO members. However, the US president had to authorize it every year, and hence it would be in the news when it was time to renew authorization.

10.2.2 *Article VI: Dumping*

This article allows a country to impose a tariff in response to unfair trade practices such as dumping by firms from another WTO member. We have discussed the economics behind dumping in Chapter 4. However, countries frequently impose anti-dumping duties against firms from other countries, mainly to protect domestic firms against foreign competition.

10.2.3 *Article IX: Provision against quantitative restrictions*

GATT/WTO prohibits the use of quantitative trade restrictions and favors restrictions in the form of tariffs (anti-dumping duties, countervailing duties, etc.). One major exception to this general rule was the multifibre agreement (MFA) organized under the aegis of GATT in 1974. This allowed industrial countries to restrict the import of textiles and apparels from less developed countries by imposing a quota. MFA specified the quantity of each textile product that each developing country could sell to the US, Europe and Canada.

Under the Uruguay round of negotiations, less developed countries were able to negotiate an end to these quotas and the MFA expired on January 1, 2005. However, in the immediate aftermath of the expiration of the MFA, there was a surge in the export of textiles and apparels from quota countries to the US, EU and Canada. To cite an example, the exports of Chinese tights and pantyhose to the EU increased by 2000% in January–February 2005, compared to a year earlier. Similarly, the Chinese exports of pullovers and Jerseys increased by 1000%. This forced the EU to negotiate a deal with China whereby China agreed to cap its export growth at 10% per year through 2008.

10.2.4 *Article XVI: Export subsidies*

This article states that countries should notify each other of the extent of subsidies and discuss the possibility of eliminating them. During the Doha round of negotiations, agricultural subsidies were a contentious issue and no agreement was reached on phasing them out. However, in December 2005, representatives from 149 member countries of WTO met in Hong Kong to negotiate over agricultural subsidies and an agreement was reached to eliminate or reduce all such subsidies. It was agreed to abolish all agricultural export subsidies by 2013. However, indirect subsidies to agriculture such as domestic farm support programs were allowed but countries agreed to phase them out over time.

10.2.5 *Article XIX: Safeguard provisions or escape clause*

This article deals with situations where a country could temporarily raise tariffs on a particular product if the surge in imports threatens serious harm to domestic producers. This was supposed to be a safety valve protecting the long-term viability of the international trading order.

10.2.6 *Article XXIV: Exceptions to MFN in the case of FTAs and customs unions*

We discussed the MFN provision of GATT/WTO earlier, which said that a member country could not discriminate between two member countries. However, this article allowed an exception to the MFN rule in the case of FTAs and customs unions. We studied these preferential trading agreements in Chapter 9 and saw that they essentially involve discriminatory trade liberalization. That is, if two WTO members A and B form an FTA, the tariff in A goes to zero for imports coming from B but stays positive for imports coming from C. Therefore, A is violating MFN by not treating C on a par with B. However, GATT/WTO allows this exception if a subset of member countries form an FTA or a customs union.

10.3 Dispute Settlement Mechanism

One key feature of the WTO compared to GATT is a more streamlined dispute settlement mechanism. Earlier these disputes were taken to international tribunals where cases could drag on for years. Now, the WTO has a more formal and effective mechanism where a panel of experts looks at each case and decisions are reached in less than a year and, even with appeals, the final decision is reached in less than 15 months.

10.4 Concluding Remarks

While the world economy has achieved tremendous expansion of world trade since the end of the Second World War under the aegis of GATT/WTO, over the last decade or so there has been a rise in anti-globalization sentiments in several parts of the world. The starkest example of this is the election of Donald Trump as the president of the US on an explicitly anti-trade platform. After coming to power, he has imposed tariffs on many countries including allies like Canada and South Korea. He has engaged in a protracted trade war with China and his administration is trying to negotiate a bilateral agreement with that country instead of relying on the multilateral trade liberalization espoused by the WTO. Moreover, the US is playing a crucial role in defanging the dispute settlement mechanism of the WTO by blocking the appointment of judges to its appellate body. The appellate body is supposed to have seven judges, but as a result of the US blocking the appointment of judges, at the time of the writing of this chapter in December 2019, only one judge has been confirmed to the appellate body. This has significantly reduced the ability of the appellate body to hear and adjudicate appeals, thereby undermining a key feature of the WTO.

www.ingramcontent.com/pod-product-compliance
Lightning Source LLC
LaVergne TN
LVHW022222200926
848481LV00006B/2072

* 9 7 8 9 8 1 1 2 2 7 6 1 5 *